Series / Number 02-047

Interest Groups and the Foreign Policy Process: U.S. Policy in the Middle East

ROBERT H. TRICE
The Ohio State University

Library of
Davidson College

⑤ SAGE PUBLICATIONS / Beverly Hills / London

Copyright © 1976 by Sage Publications, Inc.

Printed in the United States of America

All rights reserved. No part of this book may be reproduced or utilized in any form or by any means, electronic or mechanical, including photocopying, recording, or by any information storage and retrieval system, without permission in writing from the publisher.

322.4
T823i

For information address:

SAGE PUBLICATIONS, INC.
275 South Beverly Drive
Beverly Hills, California 90212

SAGE PUBLICATIONS, INC.
St George's House / 44 Hatton Garden
London EC1N 8ER

International Standard Book Number 0-8039-0761-3

Library of Congress Catalog Card No. L.C. 76-51957

FIRST PRINTING

When citing a professional paper, please use the proper form. Remember to cite the correct Sage Professional Paper series title and include the paper number. One of the two following formats can be adapted (depending on the style manual used):

(1) AZAR, E. E. (1972) "International Events Interaction Analysis." Sage Professional Paper in International Studies, 1, 02-001. Beverly Hills and London: Sage Pubns.

OR   79-1582

(2) Azar, Edward E. 1972. *International Events Interaction Analysis.* Sage Professional Paper in International Studies, Vol. 1., no. 02-001. Beverly Hills and London: Sage Publications.

CONTENTS

Introduction 5

I. Interest Groups and the Foreign Policy Process:
   A Conceptual Framework 7
       Dimensions of Interest Group Behavior 7
       Organizational Characteristics 11
       The Structure of the Decision-Making System 11
       The Domestic Political Environment 14
       The International Political Environment 18
       Policy Issue 19
       Conclusion 22

II. Domestic Interest Groups and the Arab-Israeli Conflict,
   1966-1974 22
       A Behavioral Analysis of Interest Group Activities: Prerequisites
         for Influence 24
       Pro-Israel and Pro-Arab Interest Groups: A Comparative
         Analysis 52

Conclusions 72

Notes 73

References 75

ROBERT H. TRICE is assistant professor of political science and program advisor for Near and Middle East studies at The Ohio State University. He did his undergraduate work at the College of William and Mary, attended the University of Chicago Graduate School of Business, and received his M.A. and Ph.D. from the University of Wisconsin-Madison. Concentrating on the impact of domestic politics on American foreign and defense policy, Dr. Trice's recent publications include chapters in Oil, the Arab-Israel Dispute and the Industrial World *(1976), and* Modules in National Security Studies *(1974) as well as journal articles.*

Interest Groups and the Foreign Policy Process: U.S. Policy in the Middle East

ROBERT H. TRICE
The Ohio State University

INTRODUCTION

Political analysts have long sought a solution to the puzzle of how governments go about making foreign policy decisions. So far, we have succeeded in identifying most of the potentially important factors involved in the process (Snyder, Bruck and Sapin, 1962; Brecher, Steinberg, and Stein, 1969). However, we have yet to fit these pieces of information together to form a coherent and complete picture of how policy decisions are generated. One reason for our lack of success in theory building is that we do not yet know enough about the characteristics of the individual components involved in policymaking. This study represents an effort to help build the base of knowledge necessary to proceed with the construction of an explanatory theory of foreign policy-making. Specifically, we will concentrate our attention on a single piece of the puzzle—domestic interest groups—and attempt to describe and explain the role they play in the making of American foreign policy.

This study is divided into two sections. In section I we shall consider a number of factors that are likely to affect the behavior and influence of foreign policy interest groups in the American political system. This general conceptual framework should help analysts to account for much of the wide variation in activities and impact exhibited by different groups operating across the entire spectrum of foreign policy issues. In section II we shall adopt

AUTHOR'S NOTE: *I would like to thank Edward Sidlow, the staff of the Polimetrics Laboratory of the Department of Political Science, and the staff of the Instruction and Research Computing Center at the Ohio State University for their valuable contributions to this project.*

a more substantive focus, and attempt to describe and explain the nature and likely effects of domestic interest group activities centered around the Arab-Israeli conflict during the period from 1966 through 1974. The scope of the empirical investigation is therefore limited to exploring the policy-making roles played by a relatively large yet manageable number of domestic actors with regard to an identifiable set of important and complex issues.

We shall use parts of the conceptual framework developed in section I to guide the multimethod analysis presented in section II, with an eye to investigating how selected theoretical notions might be operationalized for purposes of empirical research. Each section has a distinctive purpose. The goal of section I is to advance our understanding of the general relationships that exist between interest groups and other elements in the policy-making process. The purpose of section II is to explore some techniques which may be useful in conducting research on the political activities of nongovernmental actors, as well as to increase our knowledge of how the complex domestic environment surrounding the making of American Middle East policy affects the behavior of governmental decision-makers. If these respective goals can be achieved we will have made progress toward the development of a viable, general model of the foreign policy process.

The term "interest group" is used to denote nongovernmental organizations—both corporations and voluntary membership associations—that engage in political activities in attempts to influence policy decisions. While interest groups are frequently mentioned as having some impact on foreign policy, there has been little systematic research on the activities they engage in or the influence they exert. The general lack of consideration paid to nongovernmental inputs can be attributed in large part to the continued concentration on the formal structure of government to characterize the decision-making process and the persistence of the monolithic national actor as a model for analyzing policy outputs. In the absence of a clear conceptual framework and systematic empirical research, the role of interest groups in the policy-making process remains for the most part an open question. Yet, if there is one set of foreign policy issues on which domestic groups are commonly assumed to have a significant impact, it is those concerning American policies toward the Arab-Israeli conflict. It is unlikely that any set of foreign policy issues has aroused such passionate and sustained public debate as has the Arab-Israeli conflict. Despite the persistence and intensity of public activity on Middle East issues, however, very little is actually known about the range of nongovernmental actors that participate or the nature and scope of their activities. And virtually nothing is known of the direct and indirect effects of their efforts on governmental policy. We shall begin the attempt to fill these investigative gaps by considering some of the important determinants of interest group behavior and impact.

I. INTEREST GROUPS AND THE FOREIGN POLICY PROCESS: A CONCEPTUAL FRAMEWORK

Our goal in this section is to develop a conceptual framework that can help us to understand more clearly where and how interest groups fit in the foreign policy-making process and in the larger domestic and international political environments within which they operate. Gable (1958: 85) is probably correct when he asserts that

> Properly the entire cultural milieu should be understood to appreciate fully the role and influence of interest groups in society. As cultural factors such as attitudes, status, and symbols vary, then the nature and function of pressure groups may vary.

However, an examination of the "entire cultural milieu" that surrounds nongovernmental actors is clearly beyond the scope of this current project. Our task will be limited to identifying a number of propositions relating selected political and social factors to interest group behavior and impact.

Our conceptual framework is built on the premise that six sets of factors can in large part explain the role on interest groups in the policy-making process. These sets of variables include:

(1) behavioral attributes of interest groups;
(2) organizational characteristics of interest groups;
(3) the structure of the decision-making system;
(4) relationships among interest groups and other actors in the domestic political environment;
(5) relationships among interest groups and other actors in the international political environment; and
(6) the policy issue.

We will now consider how each of these variable clusters is likely to affect the impact of domestic interest groups on foreign policy.

DIMENSIONS OF INTEREST GROUP BEHAVIOR

Three important assumptions undergird the attempt to establish a set of behavioral prerequisites for interest group influence. First, it is assumed that interest groups have no formal policy-making authority, and therefore that any group's impact on policy is a direct function of its ability to get relevant decision-makers to incorporate the group's preferences in a policy decision. Second, it is assumed that domestic actors must manifest their interests in observable behavior in order to have a direct effect on policy. Third, we assume that the ability of an interest group to affect policy is in large part dependent on how it attempts to have its policy preferences considered and supported by policy-makers. We will see that nongovernmental actors can contribute to policy debates in a variety of ways. However, there are four dimensions of interest group behavior that appear to be particularly important in determining how any given group or set of groups impinges on governmental policy-making. These four characteristics are:

(1) the level or amount of interest group activity;
(2) the policy objectives of the group;
(3) the timing of its actions; and
(4) the targeting strategies and techniques employed by the interest group.

Each of these four dimensions should be viewed as a behavioral continuum, with diametrically opposed attributes serving as the poles. We will describe each continuum in terms of the polar attributes, while recognizing that the actual behavior of most groups will fall somewhere between the two extremes. When combined, these attributes can be used to characterize the different types of contributions that interest groups can make to the policy-making process.

Level of Activity

The most general attribute that can be used to characterize the behavior of different interest groups is the amount or level of their political activity with regard to particular issues. At one pole are interest groups that strenuously seek access to decision-makers and push hard to have their preferences incorporated in policy decisions. We refer to these organizations as *active* interest groups. In contrast, at the other pole are those groups that make no observable effort to contribute to the policy debate on a specific issue. These actors are designated *passive* interest groups. Organizations that engage in no political activity with regard to an issue perform no policy-making role and therefore are precluded from having a direct impact on governmental decisions. Thus, the distinguishing characteristic between more active, less active, and passive actors is observable political activity. If all other factors are equal—which is a most unlikely occurrence—we would expect that the more active an interest group, the more likely it is to have some impact on policy outputs.

Policy Objectives

The level of activity is a very crude measure for characterizing the behavior of different interest groups. It is useful to the extent that it can distinguish totally passive groups from more or less active ones, but it provides no means for characterizing the policy-relevant aspects of the behavior of relatively active groups. The other three behavioral dimensions—policy objectives, timing, and targeting strategies—can account in part for the differential ability of active groups to affect policy. The success of an interest group's efforts should be related to its political goals, or in the issue-specific sense, its policy objectives. The argument is that the ability of an interest group to have an impact on policy is determined in part by *what* it is trying to accomplish.

An interest group's objective may be to see its preferences incorporated in a formal governmental decision, in which case it becomes an *advocate* of a specific policy position. Thus, an advocate develops and articulates arguments in support of the policy alternative it favors. In contrast, an interest group may seek to block a decision from being made that would run contrary to its policy preferences. In instances when groups attempt to prevent the selection of a particular policy alternative, or when they attempt to preclude certain options from even being considered, they are viewed as policy *antagonists*. In the polar case, an antagonist would offer no positive policy alternative, concentrating its actions on attacking the proposals advanced by other actors. The advocate-antagonist distinction represents the offensive and defensive sides of the political coin. While either approach may be effective in any particular situation, we would expect that over time and issues advocates would have a political advantage over antagonists to the extent that they are more likely to be viewed by policy-makers as constructive, rather than destructive, domestic forces. As a result, decision-makers are likely to be more receptive toward advocates than antagonists; depending, of course, on the perceived reasonableness and feasibility of the specific policy options advanced.

Timing

When a nongovernmental actor initiates political action may be an important determinant of its effect on policy. In the grossest sense, we can distinguish between interest groups that engage in policy-relevant activities before a decision is made and those that act after the announcement of a decision. Group activity initiated prior to the decision—that is, during the policy-making process—is *formulative* behavior, while that which follows policy pronouncements constitutes *reactive* behavior. Only formulative behavior can directly affect the process leading to any particular decision. However, reactions from interest groups can produce important but indirect effects on policy by affecting the implementation of the decision into governmental action, and by providing decision-makers with feedback that may affect the way future policy decisions are made.

Depending on the issue, the structure of the decision-making system, and the organizational characteristics of the interest group, both advocates and antagonists may adopt a formulative or reactive role. It is not uncommon, of course, for a persistent issue to be dealt with by means of a "policy" that evolves from a series of specific decisions. In such cases it may be difficult to separate formulative from reactive behavior. This problem can be minimized, however, by identifying and separately analyzing the composite decisions and the processes leading to those decisions.

Targeting Strategies and Techniques

The final behavioral characteristic that affects the impact of active interest groups is *how* they go about making their policy preferences known to decision-makers. In this study, we distinguish between direct and indirect techniques for gaining access to policy-makers (Gable, 1958: 89-90). When an interest group employs *direct techniques*, it makes its contribution to the policy debate by openly expressing its preferences to governmental actors. Direct tactics include face-to-face contacts with policy-makers, appearances before congressional committees, distribution of position papers within the government, and so on. *Indirect techniques* involve attempts to use other nongovernmental actors or elements (such as public opinion polls) as conduits for the expression of the group's policy preferences. In contrast to direct techniques, indirect political activities do not include policy-makers among the primary targets.

Most interest groups will use some mix of direct and indirect influence-seeking techniques. If a group has access to decision-makers it may supplement its direct efforts by attempting to enlist the support of other actors who have their own independent avenues of communication with government officials. However, if a group does not seek or is generally unable to gain direct access it may be forced to use indirect methods, such as mass mailings or political advertisements, as the primary means of articulating its policy preferences. Thus, while important, a high volume of formulative activity may not be adequate to ensure a group a meaningful role in the decision-making process. To be effective a group must channel its efforts in directions that will permit it to translate its political activities into decisional payoffs. Relative to a direct approach, there is likely to be considerably more slippage, diffusion, and distortion when an indirect strategy is employed and a group's policy preferences are forced to follow a circuitous route from the initiating group through various filters in the political environment to relevant policy-makers. Thus, we would expect that the more a group uses a strategy weighted in favor of directing its actions toward identifiable policy-makers, the more likely it is to have an attributable impact on decisional outputs.

The three variables—objectives, timing, and targeting strategies—represent independent dimensions of the behavior of active interest groups. Thus, on any given issue an active interest group can be either a policy advocate or a policy antagonist. In turn, both advocates and antagonists can engage in formulative or reactive behavior. And finally, both formulative and reactive activities can reflect either a more direct or a more indirect targeting strategy. In one sense, the behavioral characteristics of interest groups can serve as independent variables that can help to explain why some groups are likely to be more effective than others. In another sense, however, the behavior of any interest group must be viewed as a dependent variable; the result of complex internal factors as well as the relationships that a group has with other relevant actors in its political environment.

ORGANIZATIONAL CHARACTERISTICS

Truman (1971), Key (1961), Cohen (1957, 1959), Turner (1958), Bauer, Pool, and Dexter (1963), and others have all found internal organizational factors such as membership characteristics, the nature of the "interests" served, age, budget, formal structure, and quality of leadership to be significant determinants of the way particular interest groups go about formulating and achieving their political objectives. Because of space limitations, we cannot fully explore here the effects of each of these organizational variables on interest group behavior. However, the general argument is that the aggregation and articulation of a group's policy preferences requires some type of organizational structure that can routinize the process of distributing relevant information to, and receiving feedback from, internal and external audiences. The particular combination of organizational variables for any group is likely to be unique, and each group faces its own distinctive set of internal problems. However, to be effective a group must establish and maintain properly functioning channels of communication both internally between its leaders and its members, and externally among its leaders and members on the one hand, and other interest groups, the general public, and governmental decision-makers on the other (LaPalombara, 1964: 173). We would expect that the ability of an interest group to gain consideration and support for its policy preferences from both governmental and nongovernmental actors is directly related to its ability to communicate with those actors, and that, in turn, its ability to formulate and articulate its policy preferences is determined by its internal structure and operations.

THE STRUCTURE OF THE DECISION-MAKING SYSTEM

The *structure* of the decision-making *system* is defined in terms of the governmental and nongovernmental actors who participate in the development, advancement, choice, and defense of policy positions with regard to particular issues. The relationships and interactions among the actors in the system that ultimately lead to a policy decision define the *nature* of the decision-making *process*. The decision-making system for a particular issue is always composed of some number of governmental actors who are formally responsible for formulating or implementing the policy decision. This "core" of governmental actors, who by law, tradition, or political clout are more or less automatically included in the system, plays an important part in determining the success of other actors—whom we will label "secondary" governmental actors and nongovernmental actors—seeking an active role in the system. The only way that interest groups can have an impact on policy is through the medium of the governmental actors effectively participating in the formulation of the decision (Truman, 1971: 288). Interest groups and other nongovernmental actors are tied to governmental actors by channels of communication (Milbrath, 1967) of varying clarity and strength. Therefore, the policy-making role played by interest groups is in large part dependent on the accessibility and receptivity of relevant government officials to interest group inputs (Snyder, Bruck, and Sapin, 1962: 159-160).

For any given policy issue there is some number of governmental and nongovernmental actors who want to have a say in the decision-making process that evolves to deal with it. In most cases, inclusion in the system is contingent only on an actor making the effort to express a policy preference. The only time that interested actors outside the decision-making "core" are actually excluded from the process is when policy deliberations among core members are conducted in secret. While the decision-making system is normally open to virtually all governmental actors, there are a number of factors that determine the relative importance of different actors within the process.

Routinized procedures for handling particular types of issues help to define some minimum number of governmental actors—the "core" or "primary" actors—who normally carry the responsibility for promulgating the decision (Allison and Halperin, 1972: 45). Beyond these officials, the functional division of labor within the government, the nature and urgency of the issue, the past behavior of governmental and nongovernmental actors on similar or related issues, and the goals of those seeking access and their relationships with primary actors, all affect the weight that an actor can bring to bear in determining a policy output. In addition, formal position within the government relative to other participants, control over relevant information, and bargaining skills are some of the other determinants of individual and organizational power within the policy-making process (Allison and Halperin, 1972: 52). These factors vary from issue to issue, with the result that the primary and secondary governmental actors and the nongovernmental actors in the system will also vary in number and importance from issue to issue.

Variations in structure and process across issues hold significant implications for the policy-making role played by interest groups. As the number of core and secondary actors increases, so do interest groups' chances of finding governmental allies who will try to translate their preferences into governmental policy. The fact that there is a potentially large number of governmental actors with organizational or personal interests in a specific issue means that there are multiple points or channels within the government through which interest groups may seek access to core actors (Holtzman, 1966: 58; Dexter, 1969: 39-40). If one governmental actor is inaccessible an interest group may turn to one or more other actors. If a group is persistent it is almost always possible to find *someone* within the government who will listen to what the group has to say. But, as we have just discussed, access may not be sufficient to ensure success because all governmental actors are not equally powerful.

To be effective, interest groups must gain access to governmental actors who meet at least three criteria. The governmental target must:

(1) be a primary actor or have access to a core actor;
(2) be powerful enough to have some impact on the outputs that emerge from the policy-making process; and
(3) be willing to support the group's policy preferences.

Failure to meet any of these conditions will limit the prospects for interest group influence. Thus, the influence of any interest group on a specific issue is directly related to both the receptivity and efficacy of the governmental actor or actors to which it gains access.

The willingness of primary governmental actors to support a group's policy preferences is a crucial prerequisite for the achievement of the group's goals. There are many factors that determine an interest group's success or failure in soliciting support from individual policy-makers. Probably the most important determinant, however, is the degree of legitimacy accorded to the group and its policy position by governmental actors. Legitimacy is defined here in terms of governmental actors' perceptions of three factors:

(1) the relation of the interests of the group to the issue at hand (Bonilla, 1956: 39-40; Cohen, 1957: 218-219);
(2) the numerical and social representativeness of the group (Cohen, 1957: 66-67; Key, 1961: 503); and
(3) the propriety of the influence-seeking techniques employed by the group.

All other things being equal, the greater the legitimacy of the interest group and its cause in the eyes of the governmental target, the greater the likelihood that the governmental actor will consider and support the policy preferences of the group. Perceptions of legitimacy are the consequence of complex social processes. The interests of a nongovernmental group are more likely to be regarded as legitimate if they are generally congruent with those of the governmental target than if they are not. Compatible "frames of reference" or "ideological connections" (Cohen, 1957: 14) between an interest group and policy-makers, derived from a variety of possible sources ranging from common socialization patterns to shared short-term political goals, tend to increase the perceived legitimacy of the group, and hence its ability to garner the support of governmental actors.

A primary function of many interest groups is to develop, formalize, and communicate preferences on policy issues. The general argument of this section has been that the choice of a particular governmental actor or set of actors as the primary target of interest group communications will significantly affect the role they play in the policy-making process. Certain targets will be more responsive to the claims and demands of specific groups than others, and on given issues certain targets will carry more weight in the process than others. Moreover, interest groups are likely to approach different governmental targets in different ways, with varying degrees of success. Interest group perceptions of the receptivity of different political targets is an important factor in determining which governmental actors are selected as the direct targets of group activities (Dexter, 1969: 63). On the whole, interest groups prefer to petition targets who they believe are predisposed to support their preferences.

THE DOMESTIC POLITICAL ENVIRONMENT

There are, of course, targets other than governmental decision-makers that interest groups can select in their attempts to affect policy. All nongovernmental groups will attempt to convey their policy preferences through communication channels with one or more of three possible types of audiences:

(1) their own memberships;
(2) other groups and the general public in either the domestic or international political environment, or both; and
(3) the government in general or specific policy-makers, the group of actors that interest groups are ultimately trying to influence (LaPalombara, 1964: 173).

The domestic political environment includes a variety of actors and elements which may affect policy outputs, and interest groups represent only a small subset of these potentially important actors. With varying degrees of efficacy, all domestic actors are capable of generating and targeting their policy preferences toward governmental decision-makers. Thus, on any given issue, an interest group may find other domestic actors to be more or less independent sources of political support or opposition. Earlier we made the distinction between direct and indirect interest group strategies. Note that indirect techniques are those whereby an interest group attempts to use other elements in its political environment in order to influence policy decisions. In this section and the next we will discuss the general proposition that the amount of support that an interest group is able to generate from other actors and elements in its domestic and international environments will directly affect both its behavior and its impact on policy.

Three sets of related domestic elements are especially important in determining the nature and effectiveness of an interest group's activities on any particular issue:

(1) public opinion;
(2) the mass communications media; and
(3) other nongovernmental groups and individuals.

An interest group's decision to rely primarily on either a direct or an indirect strategy, or is more common, to select some mix of direct and indirect techniques will be shaped largely by its perceptions of the receptivity of governmental actors and the relative friendliness or hostility of the political environment within which it operates.

Public Opinion

The term "public opinion" is used to denote the general climate or distribution of opinions among the population at large on an issue or set of issues. Public opinion, as reflected in national polls, is generally passive, setting a backdrop for the more goal directed and articulate opinions of interest groups. Mass public opinion can have an impact on the policy-making process in two ways, both of which carry implications for the success of interest group efforts. First, a direct effect of opinion polls may be to create an impression of a widespread consensus on a specific solution to a policy problem, thereby establishing expectations for policy-makers as to what decisional output would be preferred by the public. If an interest group can build and control the appearance of support for its policy preferences among the general population it is likely to enhance its legitimacy in the eyes of decision-makers, thereby increasing the chances that its preferences will receive serious consideration.

A second and potentially more potent way that mass public opinion can affect the role of interest groups is by becoming part of the "cultural milieu" that helps shape the perceptions and behavior of governmental policy-makers (Cohen, 157: 29). The process by which a body of political opinion becomes so widely accepted that it is no longer the subject of meaningful debate, but rather is transformed into a cultural norm of sorts, is a gradual one. General policy orientations which attain the status of "national traditions" develop over time from a series of mutually supportive and at least reasonably successful decisional outcomes. In the absence of obvious failure, mass public opinion will tend to support the continuation of existing policies and to reinforce existing ways of approaching problems that arise in that policy area. Interest groups that are able to frame their position on a specific issue in terms of a long-standing, general policy hold an advantage to the extent that they are more likely to elicit "knee-jerk" supportive reactions from both decision-makers and the mass public alike. Obversely, groups that are seeking a reversal in a "traditional" policy orientation are at a disadvantage. The burden of proof as to why a change in policy is necessary and desirable falls on their shoulders, along with the arduous task of convincing the public that the assumptions that have underlaid its support are no longer valid.

Mass Communications Media

The mass communications media represent another set of domestic actors that can have a significant effect on the policy impact of different interest groups. The media themselves function as nongovernmental political actors when they advance or support policy positions through the editorial columns and broadcasts of political journalists (Cohen, 1973: 197). In these instances, they may become open allies or enemies of other corporate, associational, or individual nongovernmental actors. The political stands that journalists articulate may affect the opinions held by the population at large, other interest groups, and government decision-makers. By virtue of their access to media which disseminate their policy preferences to potential audiences that can run into millions of people, this relatively small group within the articulate public[1] makes up a disproportionately large segment of the key influentials whose opinions are often identified as *the* public opinion on foreign policy issues (Warwick, 1972: 320-321). Therefore, the amount of support that interest groups can muster from political journalists is likely to be important in determining how much support they will receive from other relevant domestic actors.

However, the effects of the media may be more subtle than open editorial support or rejection of an interest group's policy preferences. In their other roles as reporters of important events and transmitters of the opinions of the articulate public, the media have considerable latitude in determining what becomes "news." The extent and nature of the media coverage of the activities of different groups may be more important in enhancing or limiting their chances of having an impact on policy than the differential support they receive from political journalists. An interest group that is trying to disseminate its policy position to the general population and to decision-makers will naturally favor media coverage that casts its position in the most favorable light. However, an interest group may favor unsympathetic press coverage as an alternative to no coverage at all. Without mass media coverage, most groups, particularly associational groups, will have few means of amplifying and distributing their message beyond their memberships. Consequently, their abilities to enlist supporters from the ranks of the articulate public are necessarily constrained under conditions of inadequate media coverage.

Lack of coverage puts an interest group at a further disadvantage because it denies the group equal participation in the media-centered process by which a public opinion consensus may appear to form. When a group is ignored by the mass media, one of its few alternatives is to buy "coverage" through the costly (a half-page advertisement in the *New York Times* cost $4,000 in 1970) and generally ineffective device of the paid political advertisement (Milbrath, 1967: 250-251). On the other hand, groups that receive consistent and positive coverage from the national media enjoy a double-edged advantage. They are able to present their policy preferences to the general public in the form of news, and thereby participate at little monetary cost in the development of mass public attitudes, while at the same time gaining indirect access to decision-makers who read or view the national media.

Intergroup Relations

The nature and extent of the relationships that exist among different interest groups represent another important set of factors that can affect the ability of any given group to influence policy. In addition to searching for alternative channels of access to government officials, an interest group is likely to attempt to enlist the aid of other groups in order to broaden its base of support among the general public and to increase its numerical representativeness—and hopefully its legitimacy—in the eyes of policy-makers. In instances where there appears to be an approximate balance in the strength of competing interests, or where the only support for particular alternatives comes from scattered pockets of constituents, decision-makers are likely to feel few constraints on the policy choices they can seriously consider (Cohen, 1959: 19). However, when faced with an active coalition of nongovernmental actors whose interests in an issue appear legitimate, which appear to represent a significant proportion of the articulate public, and which appear to have generated widespread support among the general population, it becomes much more difficult for decision-makers, particularly congressmen, to ignore the policy preferences the coalition advances. What, then, are some of the tactics used by interest groups to broaden their base of support?

One common technique is for groups to petition other groups with similar political or functional interests for active support. Requests for assistance from regular allies may occur on an ad hoc, issue by issue, basis or may be part of an informal "understanding" between the leaders of separate groups, or may result from more formal ties such as interlocking directorates or common membership in an "umbrella" organization (Turner, 1958: 64-65). A second approach is to focus propaganda efforts at large but discernible groups within society—such as labor, Blacks, or Catholics—in the hope of building a broader base of mass support. Yet another way that organizations attempt to build and maintain support from their environment is by keeping close tabs on the policy stands other groups adopt, and giving positive or negative reinforcement as the case warrants.

Finally, there is another side to intergroup relations that contrasts with the reasonably cooperative nature of the interactions discussed up to this point. That is the open verbal and sometimes even physical conflict that takes place among diametrically opposed groups competing in the public arena. In instances where organizations enter into open political conflict with one another they will seek to neutralize and discredit their opponents, and will attempt to isolate them from potential sources of support in the domestic environment (Turner, 1958: 64-65). The most common tactic is to attack the logic, the motives, or the values underlying an opposing group's position.

If an interest group can get direct access to governmental decision-makers, it is still likely to seek support for its position from other domestic actors with independent channels of input into the policy-making process. If successful, the group enhances its ability to enter the system at numerous points, increases its base of public support, and stands a better chance of gaining serious consideration for its policy preferences. If unsuccessful, however, direct access may mean no more than that a single voice is provided the opportunity to compete for consideration with other actors who may carry the weight of perceived public support behind them. If the group is denied direct access and therefore must rely on indirect tactics to gain influence, its chances for success become almost totally dependent on the political interests and goodwill of other elements in its domestic environment. If it can convince other groups or the public at large that its cause is legitimate and its position is viable, it may be able to find a surrogate that does have access and that can present its policy preferences to governmental decision-makers. If, on the other hand, the group's pleas for domestic support fall on deaf ears, it will most likely be precluded from playing any meaningful role in the policy-making process.

THE INTERNATIONAL POLITICAL ENVIRONMENT

Despite the overwhelming importance of domestic political factors, actors in the international environment may also affect the decision-making role of domestic nongovernmental groups. Three sets of actors are particularly relevant: foreign governmental actors; multinational nongovernmental actors, such as "parent" or "sister" organizations in foreign countries as well as multinational corporations; and international governmental organizations. All communications between domestic interest groups and foreign or multinational actors fall under the heading of what Keohane and Nye call "transnational interactions" (1972: xii). Two aspects of transnational relations, in particular, are likely to have significant effects on the behavior and impact of domestic groups.

The first aspect is the extent of direct guidance that a domestic group gets from actors in the international environment when formulating its policy positions. A number of foreign policy interest groups attempt to coordinate their political activities with those of foreign governments in support of a particular policy line. And the behavior of a domestic group will be affected by the degree to which it serves as a "linkage" between different national political systems. A linkage is defined here as an actor that regularly performs the intermediary function of converting the outputs of one national political system into the inputs of another.[2] There are two parts involved in the performance of the linkage function:

(1) an actor must simultaneously have direct communication channels to two or more national political systems; and
(2) an actor must convert the attitudes, preferences, or policy positions generated within one system into the inputs of another system.

A linkage therefore has both a structural and a behavioral component. It is an entity—an organization or an individual—that acts to tie two or more political systems together. By definition, a domestic interest group is formally organized and conducts the bulk of its political activity in only one country However, there is nothing in this definition that precludes regular interaction between a domestic group and a foreign or multinational organization.

When a domestic interest group serves as a transnational or transgovernmental linkage, its behavior and role are likely to be different from that of an interest group operating independently and exclusively in one national political system. As a transnational linkage, a group is likely to become a medium for the expression of the policy preferences held by a foreign actor, rather than an actor advancing its own independently-generated interests. The access and consideration accorded to a group that is openly serving as a linkage will vary depending on the issue, the target's perceptions of the legitimacy of the group's linkage activities, and the content of the message conveyed. For some foreign policy issues, it may be possible for a nongovernmental actor to gain direct access to decision-makers in its role as a transgovernmental linkage that it could not achieve otherwise; while for others, policy-makers may view the opinions of foreign actors conveyed by domestic groups as illegitimate intrusions into the national policy-making process.

The second relevant aspect of transnational relations concerns the extent and nature of the political support that a domestic group can gain from foreign and multinational actors. Despite the limitations on the influence of foreign actors in the domestic political system, a domestic group may still find the support of foreign actors helpful in acquiring indirect access to policy-makers. Nongovernmental actors that find themselves with neither direct nor indirect access in the domestic environment may turn to foreign governments and interest groups as a way of getting indirect access to policy-makers through the international environment. For example, domestic groups will sometimes enlist the aid of foreign governments in publishing stories on American policy in foreign newspapers in the hope that American diplomats and intelligence personnel will relay these "foreign" analyses back to Washington where they may serve as inputs into the policy-making process. Similarly, domestic groups may on occasion write position papers to be used by foreign diplomats in their discussions with American officials. In general, a strategy that employs foreign actors to achieve indirect access will probably not be as successful as one that focuses on the support of domestic actors. For a group that is isolated in an apathetic or hostile domestic political environment, however, an attempt at indirect access through foreign actors may provide it with one of its few opportunities to play any role in the decision-making process.

POLICY ISSUE

Throughout the development of our conceptual framework we have referred to the notion of "policy issue" as a factor that helps determine the decision-making role of interest groups. A foreign policy "issue" is a recognized topic of discussion or debate centering on a particular political, social, economic, or military problem. It is, in essence, what political activities and political decisions are all about: attempts to solve problems that are important to some number of people through governmental action. The issues that we, as analysts, choose to investigate are likely to have significant effects on the conclusions we draw concerning how the "political process" works and on our ability to generalize our findings to political phenomena that we have not investigated in detail. It is likely that as the specific topic of political discussion varies, the behavior and decisional impact of nongovernmental actors are also likely to vary.

As a variable, issues can have both direct and indirect effects on the way interest groups act and their ability to influence policy outputs. The direct effects result from the fact that different issues will motivate different sets of nongovernmental actors to engage in political activities. The nature of an issue will also help determine, along with organizational characteristics, the intensity and conviction of purpose with which interest groups attempt to influence decisions. Variations in the salience of different issues may therefore help set parameters for the types and amount of effort any given group is willing to expend in its quest for policy impact. However, the indirect effects of the issue variable are often more important than the direct effects in determining the policy-making role of domestic interest groups. For as an issue affects the structure of the decision-making system, the nature of the policy process, and the domestic and international political environments, it also necessarily affects the role assumed by nongovernmental actors. Let us briefly discuss how an issue interacts with the other variables in the framework, and what the political consequences of such interactions are likely to be for interest groups.

First, each policy issue is intertwined with the structure of the decision-making that evolves to deal with it. We have argued that the functional division of labor within the government establishes routinized processes for selecting some minimum number of governmental actors that will consider and attempt to resolve particular types of problems. In addition, perceptions of the urgency or salience of an issue on the part of other government officials who have the legal or political power to become core actors will also determine the structure of the system and consequently the nature of the process. As Bauer, Pool, and Dexter (1973: 480) have noted:

> Any given issue must compete with other issues for those scarce resources which determine the outcome: time, energy, attention, money, manpower, and goodwill. Where a given issue stands in priority affects not only the fight for resources but also the whole manner of its handling. If a matter has very low priority, it gets no attention, and nature is left to take its course.

The crucial point here is that a policy "issue" can arise only after it is perceived as such by potential decision-makers. In their attempts to resolve a problem an issue-specific system will form and a policy-making process will be initiated. But, if governmental actors do not recognize a problem then there is no policy issue, and without an issue there is no system and no decision-making process.

Once an issue is "recognized" by some number of core governmental actors, the issue as perceived and defined will take on a momentum of its own and function more or less as an independent variable. But initially an issue has no life outside of that granted to it by decision-makers. Thus, what an interest group perceives as an "issue" may not be an "issue" in the eyes of governmental policy-makers. In such cases, an interest group's first step is to convince relevant officials that there is a problem that must be dealt with through governmental action. If successful, a nongovernmental group may increase its chances for exerting influence to the extent that it can define an issue in terms of its own interests, and to the extent that it can define the appropriate (and hopefully sympathetic) governmental actors that should handle it. On the other hand, if the nongovernmental group fails there will be no process and, therefore, no mechanism by which the group can influence governmental action.

Second, governmental actors' perceptions of the nature and the parameters of a recognized issue will affect the policy-making role that nongovernmental actors are allowed to play. We have argued that the consideration given to a group's policy preferences is often a function of the perceived legitimacy of the group's interest and activities with regard to the issue at hand. As a result, *how* an issue is defined and *who* the governmental actors are that are dealing with it are important in determining whether or not a group's interest in the issue is considered legitimate (Cohen, 1959: 11). If nongovernmental actors are able to identify their vital interests with the resolution of an issue as defined by the core actors, they stand a reasonably good chance of gaining access and consideration for their policy positions. However, if decision-makers define an issue in such a way that a group's interests in the matter are considered peripheral or illegitimate, its ability to affect major decisional outputs is likely to be severely limited.

Finally, the issue variable will affect interest group behavior and influence through its impact on the domestic and international political environments. In general, the salience of an issue to the population at large, to the entire range of nongovernmental actors in the domestic political system, and to foreign governmental and nongovernmental actors will affect the role of any interest group seeking to influence policy. Issues that generate widespread interest foster the proliferation of competing actors and policy positions, and are therefore often likely to diminish the influence that any one actor or set of actors can exert (Milbrath, 1967: 249). However, under certain conditions interest groups may be able to use widespread public interest to their political advantage. To the extent that a group can neutralize and isolate competing groups, and can enlist the support of other actors in the domestic and international environments, it may be able to broaden its base of public support and gain indirect access to policy-makers. On the other hand, governmental actors dealing with issues that are salient only to a small number of domestic actors may be relatively more accessible and willing to consider group preferences because of the ability of the groups to identify their primary interests with the outputs of the decision-making process.

CONCLUSION

The variables in the conceptual framework should be useful in explaining why any given interest group behaves as it does, and in assessing the likelihood that the group will see its policy preferences translated into governmental action. We have seen that the variable clusters—behavioral characteristics, organizational characteristics, the structure of the decision-making system, group relationships with the domestic and international environments, and the policy issue—are interrelated in complex, and sometimes almost circular ways. What may be viewed from one perspective as an independent variable affecting the policy impact of a group, may be seen from another angle as a dependent variable. Thus, the importance of any explanatory factor in the framework is likely to be a function of the questions that analysts ask, and the additional assumptions and biases they carry into the research situation. The utility of any conceptual framework must be judged primarily by its ability to help us better understand reality. But before we can explain reality we must first describe it. And the way that we simplify reality for purposes of description holds significant consequences for our ability to explain it. If our operational definitions of political phenomena diverge too far from the intuitively plausible and satisfying notions in our conceptual frameworks, we run the risk of generating empirical results which on the one hand are artificial, and on the other are inexplicable with existing theories. In section II, we will try to be sensitive to the problems that necessarily accompany systematic attempts to describe and explain political reality.

II. DOMESTIC INTEREST GROUPS AND THE ARAB-ISRAELI CONFLICT, 1966-1974

In this section we will adopt a more substantive orientation and focus in some detail on domestic interest group activities related to the Arab-Israeli conflict during the period from 1966 through 1974. Specifically, we will attempt to achieve three research objectives. The first goal is to provide a reasonably clear picture of both the sources and nature of domestic inputs into the American policy-making process on Arab-Israeli issues. The second objective is to consider relative strengths and weaknesses of some of the methodological approaches commonly used in foreign policy analysis. And the third and most important goal is to apply a number of the propositions developed in section I, and see how well they are able to explain variations in the behavior and likely influence of selected domestic groups. With the conceptual framework serving as a general guide, we will use the behavior patterns and the relationships uncovered in the descriptive analysis that follows to generate some expectations concerning the potential ability of interest groups in general—and pro-Israel and pro-Arab interest groups in particular—to have an observable impact on American Middle East policy.

Throughout the empirical analysis we will be searching for behavioral and relational characteristics that maximize the likelihood that interest group activities will affect the behavior of policy-makers, and hence decisional outputs. Unfortunately our findings must be couched in terms such as "likely influence" and "potential impact" because our expectations can be neither confirmed nor dismissed until a viable measure is found for the primary dependent variable—impact or influence. Finding a solution to the age-old problem of measuring influence is beyond the bounds of this endeavor. Rather than attempt to resolve the debate, we will approach the notion of observable interest group impact by asking the following question: Does it appear likely that the behavior of governmental policy-makers responsible for the formulation of a given policy decision would be any different because of interest group input than the behavior that we, as analysts, would expect in the absence of domestic group activity? That is, given interest group activity in the domestic environment, does it appear likely that such activity will affect the way policy-makers consider, resolve, or shelve a particular policy problem? To the extent that decision-makers appear likely to react specifically to interest group stimuli, interest groups can be said to play some observable role in the policy-making process.

The analysis is divided into two parts, and reflects a multimethod approach to the study of interest groups and the foreign policy process. In part I, events data are used to characterize interest group activities along a number of the dimensions outlined in the conceptual framework. Findings from the behavioral analysis are supplemented by qualitative analyses of relevant groups and activities. In part 2, we will narrow our focus and consider two sets of domestic actors—pro-Israel and pro-Arab groups—that are particularly important for understanding how American Middle East policy is made. While it will not be possible here to examine all the relationships developed in the conceptual framework, comparative analyses of the organizational structures of the pro-Israel and pro-Arab movements, and their relationships with governmental actors and other actors in the domestic environment will allow us to make some reasoned judgments concerning their relative potential abilities to affect governmental policy. Before isolating pro-Israel and pro-Arab groups for analysis, we will first consider the entire range of domestic actors that show an active interest in the Arab-Israeli conflict.

A BEHAVIORAL ANALYSIS OF INTEREST GROUP ACTIVITIES: PREREQUISITES FOR INFLUENCE

An events data [3] base has been constructed for the purpose of characterizing domestic interest group activity related to the Arab-Israeli conflict during the period from January 1, 1966 through December 31, 1974. These data will be analyzed from three distinct but complimentary angles. First, from the macroanalytic perspective interest group behavior is viewed as an undifferentiated mass of political activity. The macroscopic view blurs the distinctions among different groups and focuses on general questions such as how and why public interest in the conflict varied over time, and the degree to which specific issues received differential attention from the articulate public. Second, at the other end of the level of analysis scale, behavior is examined from a microanalytic perspective. The most active groups in the public arena are identified and singled out for discussion. Third, we will settle on a middle-level analytic perspective that clusters all groups into nine distinguishable "opinion groups." The middle-level view permits comparative analyses of the interest and behavior of pro-Israel groups, corporations, pro-Arab groups, Blacks, labor and so on. Each of these three perspectives employs a distinct unit of analysis, and each carries with it its own analytical advantages and limitations. At each level different types of questions can be asked, the answers to which can provide a partial view of interest group activities. A synthesis of the information generated from each perspective will lead to a reasonably comprehensive picture of the public's inputs on Middle East policy issues, and will provide some yardsticks by which to measure its likely impact.

Methodology

The events data analysis which follows stands in contrast to the more common interview or questionnaire approach to studying interest groups and the foreign policy process (see Bauer, Pool and Dexter, 1963; Chittick, 1970; and Cohen, 1973). The studies which have employed these more traditional techniques have produced important insights into the perceptions and attitudes of interest group leaders, lobbyists, and policy-makers. However, the descriptive and explanatory value of these works has been limited by the lack of independent data on the nature and kinds of political activities engaged in by both nongovernmental and governmental actors. Findings based on data derived from interviews or questionnaires are rarely adequate by themselves for reconstructing a complete picture of the decision-making process. Respondents' descriptions of past motives and events are by definition after-the-fact, and are often either consciously or unconsciously self-serving (Dean and White, 1970). The result is that interview data are often characterized by inconsistencies and contradictions as to who did what, when, and to whom in a given situation.

Given that one of our long term research goals is to explain how foreign policy decisions are made and the role that interest groups play in that process, it will at some point become necessary to gauge the slippage between actors' perceptions and behavior. One way of tackling this problem is to compare interview or questionnaire—derived data with data concerning the activities of relevant actors drawn from publicly available sources. Of course, data on behavior taken from public sources carry with them their own set of problems (see Azar, 1975). The point remains, however, that we must know both how interest groups behave as well as how they and other perceive and evaluate their actions before we can begin to understand their impact on foreign policy. The events data approach employed in this section, therefore, represents only one aspect of the larger multimethod undertaking necessary to understand the foreign policy role of domestic interest groups.

The particular events coding schema constructed for this study is named the Political Activities of Non-Governmental Actors (PANGA) coding system (Trice, 1976b). The structure of the PANGA system draws heavily on the groundwork laid by recent events data projects (Azar, Brody, and McClelland, 1972; Burgess and Lawton, 1972; Wynn, 1973; Azar and Ben-Dak, 1975). However, virtually all events data studies in the international relations and foreign policy field have focused their attention on the behavior of international and governmental actors (two important exceptions are Brewer, 1975; and Mansbach and Lampert, 1975). The focus of this endeavor is on subnational, nongovernmental actors and not on international and governmental actors. By using events data to examine domestic inputs into the foreign policy process it is hoped that we can begin to correct an unfortunate bias that has characterized behavioral foreign policy research up to this point.

There is a relatively large amount of information available on the foreign policy-related activities of interest groups in the United States that is suitable for transformation into events data. However, it must be understood that events data represent only a sample of the behavior of the actors being studied. The information in the PANGA events file is limited to the events reported in the media source used, *The New York Times Index*.[4] As a result, the many acts initiated by domestic groups that are reported in indexed newspapers other than the *Times*, in non-indexed media sources, and those that are not reported in the public media at all, are "lost" for purposes of quantitative analysis. Thus, the behavioral generalizations drawn from analysis of the PANGA events file must be qualified by recognition of the limitations associated with the data source.

The PANGA events file covers the period from January 1, 1966 through December 31, 1974, and includes a total of 1,237 events. All events were coded by the author. There are a total of 228 nongovernmental and governmental actor/target codes in the file. Included in this list are a number of different types of actors. Among the domestic interest groups are 154 associational groups, 25 corporations, and six American political parties. There are 22 governmental targets, ranging in specificity from the president to the Department of State to the unspecified government or administration. In addition there are 21 "unspecified" actor/target codes which denote individuals or groups that either are not mentioned by name in the data source, such as a reference to "U.S. oil companies," or that defy any but the most general categorization, such as "U.S. public" or "U.S. Jews." For the most part a straightforward cross-tabulation approach has been used to describe the relevant dimensions of domestic group behavior.

The Macro-Analytic Perspective

Our first view of interest group activities will be from the analytical equivalent of a wide angle lens. Such a perspective provides the broad outlines of the political landscape and directs attention toward those features that deserve closer examination. In this section we attempt to get a "feel" for the domestic environment by addressing the following questions: How has the interest of the articulate public in the Arab-Israeli conflict, as reflected in observable activity, varied over time? How has support or criticism of the major parties to the conflict been reflected in interest group activities? How has public interest in the different issues which together comprise the "Arab-Israeli conflict" varied over time? And has public support for the major parties to the conflict varied from issue to issue?

Figure 1 displays the total level of public interest group activity related to the Arab-Israeli conflict, by year from 1966 through 1974. The yearly totals include nongovernmental actor messages to the public at large, group to group interactions, and interest group actions targeted at governmental officials. The significant feature of Figure 1 is the wide variation in the level of domestic activity across the nine years. The proportionately low level of activity that characterized 1966 is representative of the generally low interest in the Middle East during the decade between the Suez Crisis of 1956 and the June War of 1967. The long crisis leading up to the June War, the stunning victory of Israel over the Arab countries, and the number and complexity of new political issues that arose in the aftermath of the war sparked a significant increase in domestic activity that was generally sustained for four years. Public interest was especially high during 1967, the year of the June War, and in 1969-1970, when intense controversy swirled around the United States' attempts to work out a peace settlement (the Rogers Plan) and the American decision to resume the sale of jet fighter-bombers to Israel. What was to be a two and one-half year lull in domestic activity began in 1971, reflecting not so much the resolution as the routinzation of many of the issues that had grown out of the June War.

Many of these controversial issues—the status of Arab refugees, United Nations and American peace-making efforts, American military and political support for Israel—became highly salient once again in the context of the October War of 1973. In addition, a whole new crop of issues—ranging from the treatment and release of Arab and Israeli POWs to the oil embargo to the UNESCO actions against Israel to the increase in P.L.O. guerrilla activities to

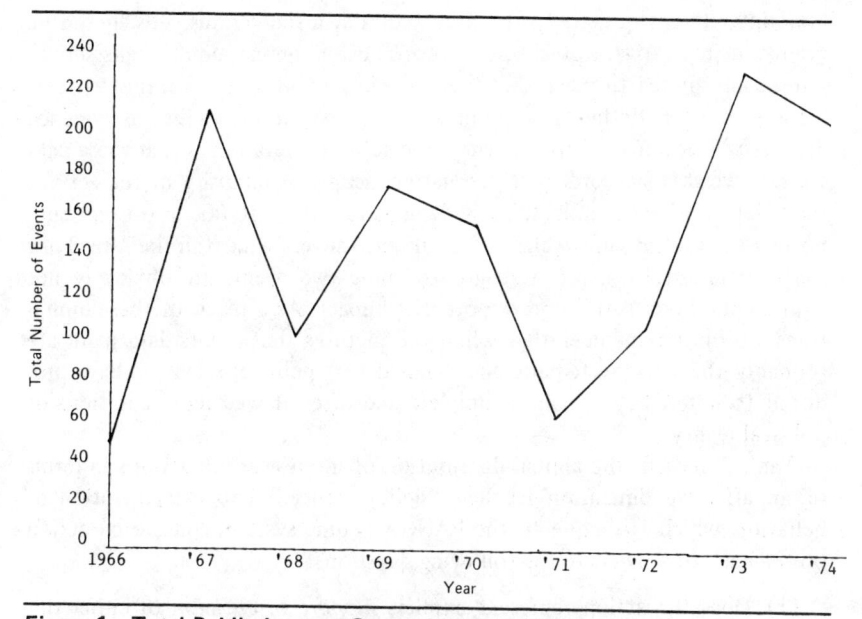

[Figure 1: line graph showing Total Number of Events by Year from 1966 to 1974]

Figure 1: Total Public Interest Group Activity, 1966-1974, by Year

Yasir Arafat's appearance at the United Nations to Joint Chiefs of Staff General Brown's unfortunate comments about American Jewry—provided new fodder for intense public debate which was reflected in high levels of activity throughout 1974.

It is important to recognize, however, that the process of policy-making goes on even when—some would say *only* when—public debate is *not* intense. Executive branch decision-makers grapple daily with the entire range of Middle East problems under varying conditions of public scrutiny. When general interest in the area periodically rises or when specific issues become topics of heated domestic political debate it is likely that the nature of the political constraints operating on decision-makers changes. On the basis of Figure 1, we might well expect variations in the impact of domestic factors on the substance of particular policies to the extent that domestic "pressures" are perceived by policy-makers as more visible or more "real" during some periods rather than others.

Given that public interest in the conflict varies over time, are there, nevertheless, clear patterns of political sentiment that could serve as general guidelines for policy-makers? Who among the major parties to the Arab-Israeli conflict enjoys the support or bears the burden of criticism of the articulate public in the United States? Has the extent of support of criticism of various parties changed over time? Table 1 provides some answers to these questions. However, in interpreting this table and those that follow two caveats must be kept in mind. The first is that because these data represent only a sample of total interest group activity the event counts in the various cells should be evaluated in relative, not absolute, terms. For example, empty cells should not be interpreted to mean that there was in fact no activity on that variable for a given year. Rather, low count or empty cells should be seen as evidence of *relatively* lower levels of activity. The second limitation is that these data are not weighted according to the nature, scope, or intensity of the actions they depict. For example, a mass demonstration of 10,000 pro-Israel supporters carries the same weight as a half-page advertisement in the *New York Times* paid for by a pro-Arab group. These two events are obviously not equivalent in terms of scope or potential impact. As a result of these limitations we must remember that while the pictures that events data paint are probably the most systematic and detailed that political scientists have produced to date, they remain incomplete and often flawed representations of political reality.

Table 1 records the annual distribution of interest group actions in terms of an affective dimension labelled "policy stance." This categorization of behavior, which is unique to the PANGA coding system, codes each action on the basis of answers to the following questions:

(1) Does the action represent explicit *support* or *criticism* of either the stated policy position or the reported actions of the referent at the time the event is initiated?

(2) If the event includes no explicit reference to a policy or an action, is the position advanced by the domestic actor *contended to be in the best interest* (and therefore supportive) of a particular referent?

Coding each event according to policy stance facilitates the recognition of the political motivations, although not the intensity of motivations, that underlie observable behavior. It permits the distinction to be made between the direct *target*—the person or group that actually "receives" the message— and the *referent* or *subject* of an act—the person, group, or nation on which the event is focused. For example, if the president of Hadassah, the Women's Zionist Organization, addresses the delegates to the annual convention and attacks P.L.O. guerrilla activities, she is initiating a "conflictual" act. But is she engaging in negative behavior toward the direct targets of her address, the delegates? Quite obviously not. While the direct targets must be coded as the delegates, her critical remarks refer to the *subject* under discussion, namely the activities of the P.L.O. Consequently, the policy stance dimension of this event would be coded "critical of P.L.O." Conventional coding systems[5] would be caught in the trap of having to code the actor, target, and the nature of the event in such a way that the political significance of the act is lost. The notion of policy stance resolves this problem by extending the "who-says-what-to-whom" question normally addressed in event coding systems to ask "who-says-what-to-whom-*about whom-and with what affect.*"

TABLE 1
Policy Stances of Domestic Interest Groups, 1966-1974, by Year

POLICY STANCE		1966	1967	1968	1969	1970	1971	1972	1973	1974	Row Sub-Totals	Row as % of Total
Support Israel	N	12	74	14	31	35	14	12	38	20	250	
	%	4.8	29.6	5.6	12.4	14.0	5.6	4.8	15.2	8.0	100	20.3
Support Arabs**/ Arab Governments	N	1	9	8	9	1	0	0	12	7	47	
	%	2.1	19.2	17.0	19.2	2.1	0.0	0.0	25.5	14.9	100	3.8
Support U.S.	N	9	5	2	2	7	0	1	12	2	40	
	%	22.5	12.5	5.0	5.0	17.5	0.0	2.5	30.0	5.0	100	3.2
Support P.L.O.	N	0	0	1	4	8	2	4	1	10	30	
	%	0.0	0.0	3.3	13.3	26.7	6.7	13.3	3.3	33.3	99.9*	2.4
Support U.N.	N	0	1	0	1	0	0	0	7	1	10	
	%	0.0	10.0	0.0	10.0	0.0	0.0	0.0	70.0	10.0	100	0.8
Criticize Israel	N	1	19	9	17	8	1	12	8	7	82	
	%	1.2	23.2	11.0	20.7	9.8	1.2	14.6	9.8	8.5	100	6.6
Criticize Arabs/ Arab Governments	N	3	3	9	44	3	3	6	29	18	118	
	%	2.5	2.5	7.6	37.3	2.5	2.5	5.1	24.6	15.3	99.9*	9.5
Criticize U.S.	N	7	8	17	11	18	11	2	13	22	109	
	%	6.4	7.3	15.6	10.1	16.5	10.1	1.8	11.9	20.2	99.9*	8.8
Criticize P.L.O.	N	0	0	3	3	7	0	13	5	29	60	
	%	0.0	0.0	5.0	5.0	11.7	0.0	21.7	8.3	48.3	100	4.9
Criticize U.N.	N	2	2	1	3	0	0	0	3	38	49	
	%	4.1	4.1	2.0	6.1	0.0	0.0	0.0	6.1	77.6	100	4.0
Neutral	N	4	18	8	7	10	2	2	13	4	68	
	%	5.9	26.5	11.8	10.3	14.7	2.9	2.9	19.1	5.9	100	5.5
N and % of Total Year's Activity	N	39	139	72	132	97	33	52	141	158	863	
	%	89.0	66.5	77.4	78.6	63.8	60.0	53.1	64.7	79.0		69.8
Other Referents	N	5	70	21	36	55	22	46	77	42	374	
	%	11.0	33.5	22.6	21.4	36.2	40.0	46.9	35.3	21.0		30.2
Column Totals	N	44	209	93	168	152	55	98	218	200	1237	
	%	100	100	100	100	100	100	100	100	100		100.0

*Due to rounding error.
**Includes Palestinian Arabs.

A comparison of the row totals in Table 1 shows differences in the aggregate levels of domestic support and criticism for selected actors across the entire nine year period. Among the more interesting findings are the following:

(1) When viewed as a whole, interest group activity is fairly evenly divided between supportive (30.5 percent total) and critical (33.8 percent total) actions. However, this generalization masks significant differences in interest and support for particular parties to the conflict;

(2) Israel was by far the most frequent single referent of domestic activity, and received substantially more relative support for its actions and policy positions than any other referent;

(3) Over the nine year period domestic activity focused much less on the Arab states and the Palestine Liberation Organization than on Israel, and tended to be much more critical than supportive of the Arab governments and the Palestinians;
(4) American policies and actions were relatively less salient than those of either the Israelis or the Arabs, and tended, on balance, to elicit relatively more criticism than support from American interest groups;
(5) The United Nations' role in the Middle East was much more likely to be attacked than supported when interest groups turned their attention relatively infrequently toward the U.N.

Looking at the individual row cells in Table 1 permits comparison of changes in relative levels of critical and supportive acts for particular referents across time, and provides a more dynamic view of interest group activity. Among other things, a year by year comparison shows that:
(1) While publicly recorded supportive activity for Israel was highest during the two periods of violent international conflict, the relative level of supportive activity was substantially lower in 1973 than it was in 1967;
(2) While observable interest group support for the Arab states remained small in terms of numbers of actions, there was a significant increase in the relative level of supportive activity between the 1967 war and the 1973 war;
(3) The appearance of Yasir Arafat at the United Nations in 1974 provoked a sharp rise in both critical and supportive actions concerning the P.L.O., and generated a sharp increase in domestic criticism of the United Nations. It is likely that 1974 signalled the emergence of both the P.L.O. and the United Nations as primary subjects of extended domestic debate in the United States.

The various parties to the conflict listed in Table 1 were the subjects of roughly 70 percent of the total number of events initiated over the nine year period.[6] While there are hints in the data that some actors, such as the U.N. and the P.L.O., may get more attention in the future than in the the past, and that the extent of nongovernmental support for some actors may be shifting, they are only hints. On the basis of publicly recorded behavior alone, the conclusion is that the dominant policy stance of the articulate public has been one of general and very strong support for Israel relative to that exhibited for relevant Arab states, the P.L.O., the United States, and the United Nations.

While helpful in characterizing general trends, the fact that undifferentiated group activity shows various levels of interest and support for the major parties to the dispute is of only limited utility in helping to sketch the potential role that domestic actors may play in the foreign policy process. These trends in sentiment are likely to act as constraints on policy-makers only in the broadest sense of establishing wide parameters for what is "acceptable" governmental policy from the point of view of the articulate public. For interest groups to affect the substance of particular policies it is likely they would have to mobilize and target their policy preferences not only on general policy but also on more specific governmental decisions. Decision-makers, especially executive branch officials, are likely to perceive themselves as having varying degrees of flexibility in the making of specific decisions to the extent that different issues arouse varying degrees of interest and debate in the domestic environment. Moreover, the relationship between policy-makers' perceptions of freedom of action and public interest is likely to be negative. That is, the higher the level of domestic interest and activity on a specific topic of policy debate, the more likely it is that decision-makers may feel that the range of viable policy options is constrained. As a result, it is important to find out which of the many aspects of the Arab-Israeli conflict are most salient to domestic interest groups. Those specific issues that attract widespread public attention are likely candidates for further, qualitative analysis on the more general and intriguing problem of how and where interest group "fit" in the policy-making process. Conversely, the potential role and impact of the articulate public is likely to be less for those issues on which it displays little manifest interest.

Table 2 displays the yearly level of interest group activity on some of the wide range of problems subsumed under the umbrella term "Arab-Israeli conflict," and points out the simplification that accompanies the use of the general term. For purposes of analysis it may be most useful to view the Arab-Israeli conflict as a series of related conflicts on a number of more specific problems. Another unique feature of the PANGA coding system is that each event is coded according to the particular topic of political, economic, military, or social debate on which the action was focused. These "issues" range in specificity from general, largely symbolic topics to very narrow policy questions. The issue variable increases the ability to generate a reasonably comprehensive, substantively oriented characterization of interest group behavior by further extending the questions asked about each event to determine "who-says-what-to-whom-about-whom-with-what-affect-*on what topic of debate.*"

Table 2 provides an overview of observable interest in selected aspects of the Middle East situation, and permits distinctions to be made among issues that arose and were resolved or shelved, those that surfaced sporadically across time, and those that remained in the focus of public attention for the entire period. One way of imposing some order on the information in Table 2 is to discuss various issues in terms of an arbitrarily defined three-tier hierarchy of public attention. In the first tier are the three issues that each accounted for more than 10 percent of total activity. It is important to realize that none of the issues in the first tier—which together account for nearly 40 percent of all activity—addresses any tangible problem directly associated

TABLE 2
Interest Group Activity on Selected Arab-Israeli Issues 1966-1974, by Year

ISSUE TITLE		1966	1967	1968	1969	1970	1971	1972	1973	1974	Row Sub-Totals
General Interest Group Support for Israel	N	3	55	11	22	24	10	18	34	21	195
	%	1.5	27.8	5.6	11.1	12.1	5.1	9.1	17.2	10.6	100
General U.S. - Israeli Relations	N	10	38	10	8	24	3	22	12	22	149
	%	6.7	25.5	6.7	5.4	16.1	2.0	14.8	8.1	14.8	100
General Interest Group Support for Arab States	N	0	24	9	7	17	11	9	37	25	139
	%	0.0	17.3	6.5	5.0	12.2	7.9	6.5	26.6	18.0	100
Palestinian Demand for Right of Self Determination/Palestine Liberation	N	0	0	4	10	11	2	26	1	38	90
	%	0.0	0.0	4.4	11.1	12.2	2.2	36.7	1.1	42.2	100
Arab Government Treatment of Jews/Prisoners of War	N	0	1	3	52	6	0	1	14	3	80
	%	0.0	1.3	3.8	65.0	7.5	0.0	1.3	17.5	3.8	100
U.S. Economic & Military Aid to Israel/Sales, Grants of Aircraft	N	4	1	12	5	18	6	3	7	3	59
	%	6.8	1.7	20.3	8.5	30.5	10.2	5.1	11.9	5.1	100.1*
Bargaining Positions on Israel-Arab Peace Talks	N	0	4	4	11	15	5	0	8	8	55
	%	0.0	7.3	7.3	20.0	27.3	9.1	0.0	14.5	14.5	100
U.N. Peace Keeping & Peace Seeking Efforts	N	0	3	0	2	0	0	0	8	33	46
	%	0.0	6.5	0.0	4.3	0.0	0.0	0.0	17.4	71.7	100
Arab Position Concerning the Availability of Oil (Oil Embargo)	N	0	2	0	0	0	0	0	18	15	35
	%	0.0	5.7	0.0	0.0	0.0	0.0	0.0	51.4	42.9	100
Arab Boycott of Firms Dealing with Israel/U.S. Business Relations with Israel	N	12	2	3	1	0	0	6	9	0	33
	%	36.4	6.1	9.1	3.0	0.0	0.0	18.2	27.3	0.0	100
Israeli National Boundaries/Occupied Territories	N	0	4	2	1	3	5	2	9	4	30
	%	0.0	13.3	6.7	3.3	10.0	16.7	6.7	30.0	13.3	100
Israeli Policy Concerning Annexation of Jerusalem	N	0	15	0	4	0	5	3	0	2	29
	%	0.0	51.7	0.0	13.8	0.0	17.2	16.3	0.0	6.9	100
Israeli Treatment of Arab Refugees, Arab Citizens, Arab POWs	N	0	2	6	2	3	1	3	8	2	27
	%	0.0	7.4	22.2	7.4	11.1	3.7	11.1	29.6	7.4	100
U.N. Security Council, UNESCO, Actions Toward Israel	N	5	1	1	4	0	1	1	2	9	24
	%	20.8	4.2	4.2	16.7	0.0	4.2	4.2	8.3	37.5	100
French Policy Concerning Arms Sales to Israel	N	0	0	0	8	11	0	0	0	0	19
	%	0.0	0.0	0.0	42.1	57.9	0.0	0.0	0.0	0.0	100
ANNUAL TOTALS, SELECTED ISSUES	N	34	152	65	137	132	49	92	167	185	1013
ALL OTHER ISSUES	N	10	57	28	31	20	6	6	51	15	224
ANNUAL TOTALS, ALL ISSUES	N	44	209	93	168	152	55	98	218	200	1237
	%	3.6	16.9	7.5	13.6	12.3	4.5	7.9	17.6	16.2	100.1*

*Due to rounding error.

with the conflict. Rather, each is non-specific and non-substantive. As a result, activities on these issues are likely to provide policy-makers with only the most general cues when formulating specific decisions. This first tier would include events such as mass celebrations of Israel's anniversary as a nation and counter-demonstrations by pro-Arab groups, verbal and written attacks by Jewish groups against perceived anti-Zionist activities, and demands that the president or Congress reaffirm American support for Israel's right to exist. In some sense these are not "issues" at all but residual categories for actions that cannot be classified according to more specific issue tags. That the number of actions in each is so large, however, does not represent a problem with the coding system. Rather, the relative levels of activity for these three issues accurately reflect the largely symbolic nature of much of the domestic activity related to the conflict, and the extent to which interest groups consume their time and energy generating non-specific support from other groups and the public at large, and attacking those groups with whom they disagree in principle.

The second tier is made up of issues that each accounted for more than 3 percent but less than 10 percent of total activity. Two activity patterns can be seen in this middle attention group. First, most of the issues tended to attract moderate levels of activity during most years, with periodic "crises" that generated brief flurries of intense activity, followed by a return to lower levels of manifest interest. Some of the issues that fall into the "recurring crisis" category are:

(1) Public interest in the activities of the Palestine liberation movement and Palestinian demands for the right of self-determination, which peaked following the attacks at the 1972 Olympics in Munich and Arafat's address to the U.N. General Assembly in 1974;

(2) Public debate concerning American aid to Israel, particularly the sale of Phantom jets, which followed the initial Israeli request for F-4s in the winter of 1967-1968, and the second request which came in early 1970;

(3) Evaluations of the bargaining positions of both Israel and the "front line" Arab states on the prerequisites and form of peace negotiations, which were most frequent during 1970 when both the first and second phases of the Rogers Plan were being considered.

Second, some issues in this tier were essentially "one shot" issues, characterized by intense public activity of relatively short duration. Thus, the efforts of the United Nations to help resolve the conflict received very little attention until the Fall of 1974 when the chairman of the Palestine Liberation Organization was permitted to address the General Assembly. Similarly, the treatment of Jewish citizens in Arab states exploded as an issue in January 1969, when the Iraqi government announced the execution of a number of Iraqi Jews for allegedly spying for Israel. Throughout 1969, undeterred by overwhelmingly negative world reaction, Iraq periodically announced the hanging of another group of alleged spies. Each announcement would elicit condemnations from both domestic groups and American government officials. It is likely that this pattern would have continued had not the Iraqis executed most of the convicted spies by the end of the year. As it was, public attention waned soon after the cessation of the hangings.

On a smaller scale the "recurring crisis" (such as, annexation of Jerusalem and the Arab boycott) and "one shot" (such as, Arab oil embargo and French arms sales policies toward Israel) activity patterns also characterize group behavior on the issues in the third attention tier, those accounting for less than 3 percent each of total activity. For these issues, however, even sporadic interest was at best moderate in intensity, with little or no public activity during most periods. It is important to note that with the exception of American arms sales policies and the bargaining positions of Israel and the Arab states on peace negotiations, virtually all of the more substantive issues that policy makers deal with on a daily basis and that must be resolved if there is ever to be peace in the Middle East (such as, the status of Jerusalem, Israeli occupation and settlement of Arab lands, increasing Israeli isolation within the United Nations, the Arab boycott of firms dealing with Israel, Israeli policy toward Arab refugees, and so on) reside in this low attention tier. Table 2 shows that this set of important issues aroused inconsistent and relatively low levels of activity on the part of the articulate public. Only spasmodically did interest groups mobilize on these issues, and even then they tended to react to announcements of policies that had already been formulated and implemented. To the extent that interest groups tend to focus their activities more on general and largely symbolic issues and devote relatively less attention to many of the narrower issues on which policy-makers must make specific decisions, it is less likely that the public exerts a significant, direct impact on many aspects of American Middle Eastern policy.

On the basis of Table 1 we concluded that interest group activity as a whole tended toward relatively greater support for Israel than for any other major actor. It might then be possible to look at the results of Table 2 and argue that it probably makes little difference that many issues received scant attention from the articulate public since domestic inputs would be likely to support Israel in any case. Thus, if policy-makers *were* trying to anticipate the policy preferences of the articulate public, they could simply interpolate from the general trends of sentiment and assume that support for Israel is as consistent across issues as it is across time. Table 3 shows the fallacy of such an argument by displaying the differential levels of support that various parties to the conflict received for a number of specific issues. This final view from the macroscopic perspective conveys the problems associated with attempts to characterize the domestic political environment in terms of simplistic generalizations. When looked at across all issues and across the entire period it is apparent that support for Israel was a dominant characteristic of American interest group activity. However, as Table 3 clearly shows, on any given issue the array of forces and the degree of support for the various parties may deviate considerably from the norm.

The nature of the policy inputs coming from the domestic environment looks much more complex when analyzed on an issue by issue basis. We can see that the commonly held notion of an articulate public ready and willing to give "knee-jerk" support to Israel on any issue may need reexamination. Table 3 shows that on specific issues the public has been reasonably selective in choosing which party to support or criticize, and has not shied away from attacking certain Israeli policies. While Israel received strong support from American interest groups in its quest for U.S. economic and military aid and the acquisition of sophisticated weaponry, it received much less support for its position of holding on to captured Arab territories. In relative terms, Israel elicited generally negative reactions from the American articulate public on certain aspects of Israeli military policy, particularly its retaliatory raid policy (such as the Es Samu attack and the Beirut airport raid), Israeli treatment of Arab refugees, and the Israeli government's decision to annex East Jerusalem after the 1967 war.

From the point of view of policy-makers, the signals coming from the public on any given specific issue may either appear "mixed," with no clear policy preference emerging from debates in the domestic environment, or may run contrary to prevailing general sentiments. On those issues where countervailing opinions tend to offset each other, or where general interest and activity is relatively low, policy-makers are apt to perceive fewer domestic constraints on their freedom of action. Tables 2 and 3 show that this combination of factors characterizes the domestic inputs on a number of important issues related to the conflict. To the extent that interest group activity focuses more on general rather than specific issues, and that the policy preferences of the articulate public as a whole are often garbled on specific issues, it is less likely that nongovernmental groups play a meaningful role in the foreign policy process.

The macro-analytic view has provided a broad picture of the political activities of the articulate public. Using aggregate level data we have made some generalizations about what a large number of organizations in the United States saw as the most important aspects of the Arab-Israeli conflict, which parties to the conflict they sought to support or criticize, and how the support of domestic groups varied over time and from issue to issue. But the simplicity and homogeneity of macro-level analysis is deceiving, for it hides all the interesting distinctions among different interest groups. By itself, aggregate analysis is incapable of providing a picture of what the relevant domestic environment of American foreign policy-makers actually looks like. In order to get a sense of the different types of actors that inhabit this environment, and their behavior, we shall slide all the way down the level of analysis scale to the micro-analytic level.

The Micro-Analytic Perspective

This section focuses on that subset of groups that was probably most important in determining the nature of public debates on Arab-Israeli issues (see Trice, 1976a). Although there were at least 185 distinct organizations that engaged in relevant activities at least once during the nine-year period, the vast majority gave only marginal and sporadic attention to the conflict. Most groups displayed an interest in only a very narrow range of issues, and most made no attempt to influence directly any policy decisions.

TABLE 3
Policy Stances of the Articulate Public on Selected Issues, 1966-1974

ISSUE	POLICY STANCE	Support Israel	Support Arab League	Support P.L.O.	Criticize Israel	Criticize Arab League	Criticize P.L.O.	Neutral	Subtotals	Other	Totals
U.S. Economic & Military Aid to Israel/Sales, Grants of Aircraft	N	32	0	0	5	0	0	1	38	21	59
	%	54.2	0.0	0.0	8.5	0.0	0.0	1.7	64.4	35.6	100
Israeli Military Policy/ Attacks on Arab States	N	11	0	0	21	0	0	0	32	7	39
	%	28.2	0.0	0.0	53.8	0.0	0.0	0.0	82	18	100
Israeli Treatment of Arab Refugees, Citizens, POWs	N	0	2	0	15	0	3	4	24	1	25
	%	0.0	8.0	0.0	60.0	0.0	12.0	16.0	96	4	100
Israeli National Boundaries/ Occupied Territories	N	11	2	0	10	1	0	1	25	5	30
	%	36.6	6.6	0.0	33.3	3.3	0.0	3.3	83.3	16.7	100
Israeli Policy Concerning Annexation of Jerusalem	N	10	0	0	13	0	0	2	25	4	29
	%	34.5	0.0	0.0	44.8	0.0	0.0	6.9	86.2	13.8	100
Military Policy of Arab States/ Attacks on Israel	N	2	4	0	0	17	0	0	23	4	27
	%	7.4	14.8	0.0	0.0	63.0	0.0	0.0	85.2	14.8	100
Palestinian Demand for Right of Self Determination	N	1	0	23	1	12	48	0	85	5	90
	%	1.1	0.0	25.6	1.1	13.3	53.3	0.0	94.5	5.5	100
Arab Governments' Treatment of Jews/Prisoners of War	N	15	0	0	1	55	1	3	75	5	80
	%	18.8	0.0	0.0	1.3	68.8	1.3	3.8	93.8	6.2	100
Arab Position Concerning the Availability of Oil (Oil Embargo)	N	2	7	0	0	16	0	0	25	10	35
	%	5.7	20.0	0.0	0.0	45.7	0.0	0.0	71.4	28.6	100

The Arab-Israeli conflict was peripheral to the primary organizational interests of most groups, and most were motivated to act only when some specific issue impinged on the policy goals of the group or when the interests of its members were directly challenged. For example, the only action initiated by the American Physiological Society was to protest the retention of one of its members as a hostage by the Popular Front for the Liberation of Palestine. Similarly, the American Travel Agent Society's single encounter with the conflict was to appeal to the Algerian government to release the passengers and crew of a hijacked El Al airliner. Many more examples could be cited to support the point that while the actions of many groups are legitimately related to the Arab-Israeli conflict, the narrowness of their interests and their lack of sustained activity make them unlikely candidates for having any significant, attributable effect on American policy.

More than 90 percent of the interest groups that participated in the public discussions and debates associated with the conflict did so on a sporadic, ad hoc basis. Of the 185 groups that engaged in publicly recorded activities, only 18 accounted for more than 1 percent each of total activity. Table 4 lists in rank order the 18 most publicly active interest groups. We can see from Table 4 that no one group dominated the political action. Rather, organized group activity related to the conflict is distinguished by the very large number of actors that displayed only passing interest in the issues involved. If we are looking for the leaders or pace-setters of the articulate public on the Arab-Israeli conflict, we will find them among the groups listed in Table 4. These 18 groups generated about 49 percent of the total actions, and were generally responsible for bringing issues to the attention of other members of the articulate public, governmental decision-makers, and the general public. For most issues, they set the tone of public debate, defined the policy alternatives (in keeping with their own policy preferences), and then formed and led loose coalitions of like-minded groups in support of their policy positions.

The pro-Arab Action Committee on American Arab Relations (ACAAR) was the single most active interest group during the 1966-1974 period. However, among the most active groups, only the anti-Zionist American Council for Judaism, the pro-Arab Association of American-Arab University Graduates, and the anti-Zionist-leaning Black coalition, the National Black Political Convention, could be counted as potential allies. Consistently, and almost single-handedly, ACAAR attempted to present the "other side" to the positions advanced by pro-Israel groups. If there was an Israel Independence Day parade and celebration in New York City, ACAAR would usually be there with a small group to counter-demonstrate. When Jewish groups would march in favor of the sale of jets to Israel, ACAAR would demonstrate in opposition to the sale. Two points should be noted in assessing the potential impact of ACAAR. First, ACAAR's high level of activity can in large part be accounted for by the antagonistic role it played toward pro-Israel groups. Second, the Action Committee's generally negative reactions to pro-Israel initiatives often limited its ability to formulate and advance positive policy suggestions of its own. The result was that ACAAR's generally reactive approach to politics, its sometimes extreme tactics, and its isolation and lack of support from other groups tended to offset the political advantages gained from its extensive public activities.

The other most active groups represent various types of ethnic and political organizations that showed a public interest in the conflict. Thus 12 of the remaining 17 are Jewish organizations. The independent-minded American Jewish Committee and the American Jewish Congress represent the non-Zionist Jewish "establishment" in this country, while the Zionist Organization of America represents the Zionist "establishment." The Conference of Presidents of Major American Jewish Organizations—more commonly called the "Presidents Conference"—is the "umbrella" group responsible for coordinating the activities of more than 30 Jewish groups on virtually all foreign policy issues. All the most active Jewish organizations except the American Jewish Committee and the Jewish Defense League are members of the Presidents Conference. When Jewish leaders meet with foreign leaders or members of the executive branch to discuss Middle East problems, the chairman of the Presidents Conference usually heads the delegation and serves as its spokesman. The Presidents Conference, which had no counterpart on the pro-Arab side until 1972,[7] is only one institutional device that traditionally has allowed proponents of pro-Israeli positions to voice their opinions with a unity and forcefulness that their opponents lack.

TABLE 4
Rank Order Listing of Most Active Interest Groups, 1966-1974

Rank	Name	Opinion Group Classification	Total N Events	% Total Activity
1	Action Committee on Arab American Relations	Pro-Arab	82	6.6%
2	Anti-Defamation League of B'nai B'rith	Pro-Israel	60	4.9
3	Conference of Presidents of Major American Jewish Organizations	Pro-Israel	60	4.9
4	American Jewish Committee	Pro-Israel	59	4.8
5	American Jewish Congress	Pro-Israel	58	4.7
6	Zionist Organization of America	Pro-Israel	53	4.3
7	Jewish Defense League	Pro-Israel	46	3.7
8	National Council of Churches	Christian/Neutral	25	2.0
9	B'nai B'rith	Pro-Israel	22	1.8
10	Rabbi Board (of New York)	Pro-Israel	18	1.5
11	Association of American-Arab University Graduates	Pro-Arab	17	1.4
12	A.F.L.-C.I.O.	Labor	16	1.3
13	American Israel Public Affairs Committee	Pro-Israel	51	1.2
14	American Council for Judaism	Anti-Zionist	14	1.1
14	Synagogue Council of America	Pro-Israel	14	1.1
14	United Jewish Appeal	Pro-Israel	14	1.1
17	Rabbinical Council of America	Pro-Israel	13	1.1
17	National Black Political Convention	Black	13	1.1
	Totals		609	49.2%

The Anti-Defamation League of B'nai B'rith (ADL)—which is a separate organization with no formal ties to the more socially oriented B'nai B'rith—is distinctive among the most active groups in that its policy interests are much more constricted than the others. Specifically concerned with protecting the human and civil rights of all Jews, ADL arose as the leader of the American outcry to the Iraqi executions of alleged Jewish spies in 1969, led the campaign for the release of Israeli POWs after the 1973 war, and has been one of the more outspoken critics of United Nations' actions against Israel since the October War. The ADL also serves as the watchdog for any perceived anti-Semitism, either manifest or latent, that may be infused into political debates.

A representative of the Jewish "anti-establishment" is also among the most active interest groups. The Jewish Defense League (JDL), with approximately 14,000 members, has been one of the most visible groups since the June War. The JDL employs a more activist strategy than the ADL in countering perceived anti-Semitism in the United States and abroad. Threats, coercion, and controlled violence have been standard tactics of the radical Jewish Defense League (Goodman, 1971). One of its primary targets over the years has been ACAAR, the vocal pro-Arab group. The 1966-1974 period was characterized by a constant stream of verbal assaults by JDL and ACAAR on each other, dotted with sporadic instances of physical attacks. But the Jewish Defense League did not limit the targets of its criticism solely to anti-Zionist and pro-Arab groups. A number of Jewish groups, particularly large mass-membership organizations, were also frequent targets of JDL accusations and condemnations. The Jewish Defense League's always aggressive posture, its sometimes illegal activities, and its alienation of a substantial portion of the American Jewish community has led to a political isolation similar to that suffered by the Action Committee on American Arab Relations. The result has been that a significant amount of the public activity of both JDL and ACAAR has taken place on the fringes of policy debates, generally far removed from the "mainstream" of the articulate public's discussions of issues and alternatives.

The anti-Zionist group, the American Council for Judaism, was very active during 1966 and 1967. Led by Rabbi Elmer Berger, the organization sought to counter Zionist propaganda by presenting what it contended was a "balanced" interpretation of the Arab-Israeli situation. Like ACAAR, one of the council's major problems was that so much effort was consumed in its role as rebutter of Zionist arguments that there was little time left for the generation of positive policy alternatives. The council faced another unique problem in that its constituency was predominantly both Jewish and anti-Zionist in character. Many members of the council's executive board felt that Rabbi Berger went too far in his attacks on Israel's military policies before and during the June War. Consequently, Berger was forced to leave the council, and with him went much of the drive behind the Jewish anti-Zionist faction in this country. The American Council for Judaism continued to function, but only as a shell of its former self. In 1970, Berger was named executive director of a new anti-Zionist organization, American Jewish Alternatives to Zionism. However, neither the council nor American Jewish Alternatives to Zionism has been able to recover the momentum that the anti-Zionist movement appeared to have prior to 1968.

The Board of Rabbis for the metropolitan area of New York was also quite active during the 1966-1974 period. The Rabbi Board served both as a clearing house for information for local rabbis and as an initiator of political action at the synagogue level. With its direct lines of communication to individual rabbis, and hence to a majority of practicing Jews in the United States, the Rabbi Board was successful in mobilizing large numbers of people for political action on short notice. Similar functions were performed by the other two most active Jewish religious groups, the Synagogue Council of America and the Rabbinical Council of America (Orthodox). The only other religious group and the single Christian group that took a consistently active public role was the National Council of Churches, the major umbrella organization of Protestant churches. The executive board of the National Council was often responsible for formulating and articulating the "official" position of American Protestants on key policy issues. It also served as the chief spokesman in defense of American Christians when Jewish organizations such as the Anti-Defamation League and the American Jewish Committee periodically leveled charges that Israel did not receive adequate political support from the Christian community.

The one other Jewish organization that must be singled out for discussion is the American Israel Public Affairs Committee (AIPAC). AIPAC presents the "Jewish position" to members of Congress in much the same way that the Presidents Conference does to members of the executive branch. AIPAC and the Presidents Conference are the two organizations that funnel the bulk of articulate Jewish opinion on policy issues to governmental decision-makers. The Presidents Conference serves as the chief public spokesman and link between executive decision-makers and the Jewish community on major issues, while AIPAC works on a more personal, day-to-day basis to build and maintain congressional support for Israel. Finally, Jewish social (B'nai B'rith) and fundraising (United Jewish Appeal) groups, along with the pro-Israel movement's close labor ally, the A.F.L.-C.I.O., give considerable support to the activities initiated by the more politically-minded pro-Israel groups.

Noticeably absent from the list of the most publicly active groups are any corporate actors. Despite the fact that the political situation in the Middle East during the 1966-1974 period acutely impinged on the operations of some of America's largest oil companies and financial institutions, these corporations generally declined to use the public arena to make their economic and political preferences known. Corporate political activity was confined to a small number of issues and tended to focus on economic-related problems. However, when corporate groups did formulate political positions they tended to convey their preferences to decision-makers through more direct and less public avenues of communication than most other groups.

The micro-level perspective has allowed us to identify those interest groups that form the core of the articulate public on most Arab-Israeli issues. But to focus solely on the activities of these actors is to overlook the behavior and potential impact of the vast majority of domestic groups. While the actions of specific, less active organizations are unlikely to be significant in and of themselves in affecting policy, in the aggregate they may be crucial in determining the political success of different segments of the articulate public. Having identified the leaders, we will now incorporate the less active groups into the analysis in order to examine the different bodies of opinion in the United States with regard to the Arab-Israeli conflict.

The Middle Level Analytic Perspective

A middle level analytic focus permits systematic and comparative examination of the activities of a large number of domestic actors in terms of a manageable set of "opinion groups." In this final cut at interest group behavior we will build on our earlier findings and analyze the extent of public interest, the extent of support and criticism for some of the key actors, and the strategies for conveying policy preferences displayed by a number of identifiable segments of American society. For the purposes of middle level analysis, 185 interest groups and 21 unspecified actors are aggregated into nine groupings representing major segments of the articulate public. For the most part, particular actors have been placed in one of the nine categories according to primary distinguishing characteristics provided by the groups themselves. Groups tend to use one or another of two distinct definitions of "interest group" to identify themselves. One set of domestic groups prefers to be classified according to the predominant characteristics that identify them as different types of organizations. These groups contend that the Arab-Israeli conflict is not their primary organizational interest and that they are not necessarily predisposed to favor any side or position associated with the conflict. Groupings based on common organizational characteristics rather than any general or inferred policy preferences are called *categoric* groups, and in this analysis include "business," "professional and educational," "labor," "church and neutral," "blacks" and "political parties and groups."

The second set, however, tends to emphasize general policy preferences rather than organizational characteristics as the factors which distinguish them from other actors. The criterion used for opinion groups in this set is the notion of *shared interest*, by which different groups with common values or attitudes on a particular set of problems identify with one another (Salisbury, 1975: 173-175). This criterion applies to the "pro-Israel," "pro-Arab," and "anti-Zionist" opinion groups. Thus, while most groups in the "pro-Israel" category share the organizational characteristic of having predominantly Jewish constituencies, some do not, such as Writers and Artists for Peace in the Middle East or the National Committee on American Foreign

Policy. What is shared by both Jewish and non-Jewish groups in the "pro-Israel" category is a general predisposition to support Israel on most issues. Similarly, both groups in the "anti-Zionist" category are also predominantly Jewish, but both the American Council for Judaism and American Jewish Alternatives to Zionism hold shared values which are very different from the Jewish groups included in the "pro-Israel" category. Definitional consistency would force us to lump both Zionist and anti-Zionist Jewish groups together if we stuck to a categoric definition of "Jewish" organizations, with the result that a weak but unique domestic force would be lost for purposes of analysis. Therefore, in the analysis which follows both categoric and shared interest definitions are used in order to identify the various groupings represented in a real and complex political arena.

Table 5 summarizes both the relative amount of activity initiated by each of the nine opinion groups (row totals) and the distribution of each group's actions across selected policy stance positions. Table 5 identifies which segments of the articulate public tended to dominate public discussions, and where the major elements of support and criticism for the various parties to the conflict resided in the domestic environment. In addition, a comparison of the relative amount of activity (either supportive or critical) expended on particular referents provides clues concerning which aspects of the conflict were of major interest to various opinion groups.

An examination of the row totals in Table 5 reveals that pro-Israel groups accounted for an overwhelming proportion (60.6 percent total actions) of the public activities related to the conflict. As 75 separate organizations and three unspecified actors ("U.S. Jews," "Rabbis," and "Zionists") are included in this grouping, it is by far the dominant nongovernmental voice, both in terms of numbers and levels of activity, on Middle East questions. The data in Table 5 further show that, in the simplest terms, pro-Israel groups concentrated their efforts on displaying support for Israel and attacking the policy positions or actions or virtually all other actors involved in the conflict. The "front line" Arab states, the United States government, the P.L.O., and the United Nations were all major targets of pro-Israel criticism. The relative attention paid by pro-Israel groups to domestic political concerns should also be noted. More than 15 percent of the total actions initiated by pro-Israel groups were consumed either in internecine squabbling (4.7 percent) or in attacks on pro-Arab groups in the United States.

Pro-Arab groups accounted for about 13 percent of the total domestic activity related to the conflict. In addition to being numerically weaker (21 organizations and two unspecified actors) and less organized than its pro-Israel counterpart, the pro-Arab movement's relatively modest level of public activity represents one of the more obvious drawbacks to its chances of becoming a truly competitive domestic force. Pro-Arab groups devoted relatively more effort to criticizing Israeli and American policies and countering what

TABLE 5
Selected Policy Stances of Major Opinion Groups, 1966-1974

OPINION GROUP		Support Israel	Criticize Israel	Support Arab States	Criticize Arab States	Support U.S.	Criticize U.S.	Support P.L.O.	Criticize P.L.O.	Support U.N.	Criticize U.S. Pro-Israel Groups	Criticize U.S. Pro-Arab Groups	Neutral Policy Stance	Subtotals	Other Policy Stances	Total/Opinion Group	Total/Group as % Total Actions
Pro-Israel	N	194	5	2	27	62	0	45	5	36	35	80	25	604	146	750	60.6
	%	25.9	.6	.3	3.6	8.3	0	6.0	.7	4.8	4.7	10.7	3.3	80.5	19.5	100.0	
Pro-Arab	N	2	39	24	1	27	15	2	2	0	28	3	10	156	6	162	13.1
	%	1.2	24.1	14.9	.6	16.7	9.3	1.2	1.2	0	17.3	1.9	6.2	96.3	3.7	100.0	
Church/Neutral	N	13	13	4	11	2	4	6	1	6	1	5	18	87	10	97	7.8
	%	13.4	13.4	4.1	11.3	2.1	4.1	6.2	1.0	6.2	3.4	5.2	18.6	89.7	11.3	100.0	
Business	N	4	3	13	3	3	0	0	1	0	2	2	8	48	5	53	4.3
	%	7.5	5.7	24.5	5.7	5.7	0	0	1.9	0	3.8	3.8	15.1	90.6	9.4	100.0	
Educational/ Professional	N	7	8	2	4	7	3	1	0	2	2	4	3	45	3	48	3.9
	%	13.6	16.7	4.2	8.4	16.4	6.3	2.1	0	4.2	4.2	8.3	6.3	93.8	6.3	100.1*	
Blacks	N	5	9	1	0	1	8	1	0	1	5	12	1	44	2	46	3.7
	%	10.9	19.6	2.2	0	2.2	17.4	2.2	0	2.2	10.9	26.1	2.2	95.7	4.3	100.0	
Political Groups	N	17	5	1	1	4	0	1	1	0	4	0	1	35	2	37	3.0
	%	45.9	13.5	2.7	2.7	10.8	0	2.7	2.7	0	10.8	0	2.7	94.6	5.4	100.0	
Labor	N	8	0	0	0	3	0	4	0	4	1	1	0	26	3	29	2.3
	%	27.5	0	0	0	10.3	0	13.8	0	13.8	3.4	3.4	0	89.7	10.3	100.0	
Anti-Zionist	N	0	0	0	1	0	0	0	0	0	6	5	2	14	1	15	1.2
	%	0	0	0	6.7	0	0	0	0	0	40.0	33.3	13.3	93.3	6.7	100.0	
N/Policy Stances	N	250	82	47	118	40	109	30	60	10	49	84	112	68	1059	178	1237	99.9*
% Total	%	20.3	6.6	3.8	9.5	3.2	8.8	2.4	4.9	.8	4.0	6.8	9.1	5.5	85.7	14.4	100.1*	

*Due to Rounding Error

they saw as pro-Israel propaganda generated by Jewish groups than they did in displaying support for the actions or positions of the Arab states.

Christian church groups, charitable organizations, and other "neutral" groups such as the National Council of Churches, the American Friends Service Committee, the National Council of Catholic Bishops, Freedom House, Promoting Enduring Peace, and some 12 other groups and seven unspecified actors accounted for nearly 8 percent of the total public debate. This opinion group, along with the professional and educational groups, tended to be relatively balanced in its displays of support and criticism of the major parties to the conflict. In their public activities, church and neutral groups showed both relatively greater support *and criticism* of Israel than they did for the Arab states, the Palestinians, or the American government. It is difficult to characterize the political activities of church and charitable groups. Although a considerable number of these actors were generally pro-Israeli in their public statements, there were at least two major issues on which most Christian groups sided with the Arab position. One issue was the Israeli annexation of Jerusalem after the June War. This action was viewed by many church groups as an illegal act from the start; and as the Israelis moved to consolidate their foothold by displacing Arab occupants and moving the seat of government from Tel Aviv to Jerusalem, the protests from American Christian groups became even more vocal. The second issue on which many Christian and charitable organizations attacked Israeli policy was the treatment of Arab refugees. Several charitable groups, such as the American Near East Refugee Aid, Inc. (ANERA) and the Catholic Near East Welfare Association were set up by Protestants and Roman Catholics in order to mitigate the hardships and suffering of the Palestinian refugees. The bitterness of the refugees and the degree of identification of American group leaders with their clientele were reflected in the occasional anti-Israeli rhetoric of some of the American church-related welfare groups. While these groups were ostensibly neutral on political issues a number of their leaders were openly sympathetic to the Palestinian position on the refugee question. At the level of general policy American pro-Israel groups elicited and maintained support from church organizations concerning the inviolability of Israeli political and territorial sovereignty. But across the spectrum of more specific issues American church and charitable groups tended to take a "middle of the road" approach, and on some issues—such as Jerusalem and the refugee problem—some groups tended to be highly critical of Israel.

Business groups were not particularly active in domestic discussions of the conflict, accounting for only about 4 percent of total actions initiated. When corporations did engage in public activities they concentrated their attention on explicating the policy positions of the Arab governments, and periodically reminding the American public as well as foreign policy-makers that a less than "even-handed" United States policy could jeopardize their economic interests in the area. Professional and educational groups, such as the Middle East Institute, the American Society for International Law, and the United Nations Association tended to devote the largest percentage of their public activities to discussions of the policy positions of Israel and the Arab governments and the various policy alternatives available to the American government for dealing with the conflict. Like the church and neutral opinion group, professional and educational groups could not be considered as openly supportive of any of the major parties.

While church, charitable, and professional organizations can be generally characterized as neutral political forces in the domestic environment, the same cannot be said of some of the more visible Black American groups. The most active Black groups were the militant-dominated National Black Political Convention gatherings, the Black Panther Party, and the Student Non-Violent Coordinating Committee (SNCC). All three of these organizations were strong supporters of the Palestine liberation movement and harsh critics of what they saw as Zionist propaganda activities. The Arab-Israeli dispute was a divisive issue for the Black community. The more outspoken and radical elements of the Black movement generally did not receive support from other Black groups for their pro-Palestinian, anti-Zionist positions. When asked by Jewish leaders to repudiate the actions of the Black Panthers and SNCC, the leaders of the Urban League, the NAACP, and the Southern Christian Leadership Conference (SCLC) did so. Branded not only as anti-Zionists but also as anti-Semites, and denied support from "mainline" Black groups, the Black radicals' attempts to generate a body of pro-Arab sentiment in the United States were largely unsuccessful.

Israel enjoyed considerable support from the major American political parties and groups. Both the Republican and Democratic parties had planks in the 1968 campaign platform pledging that their candidates, if elected, would grant Israel's request for Phantom jets (Porter and Johnson, 1970: 713, 725, 761); and Nixon, McGovern, and Wallace all reaffirmed America's unspecified "commitments" to Israel in 1972. On the whole the national political parties tended to emphasize the general goal of peace in the Middle East and the "special relationship" between Israel and the United States. The other, more sporadic actors such as the Communist Party of the U.S.A., the National States Rights Party (White Supremacy Party), and the Socialist Workers Party tended to be less restrained than the major parties, and more willing to show open support for either the Israelis or the Arab states. However, the contribution of all political parties to the public debate was so inconsistent relative to other opinion groups that except in presidential election years they could hardly be considered more than a peripheral set of non-governmental actors.

American labor groups, led by George Meany and the A.F.L.-C.I.O., tended to follow the lead of pro-Israel groups on virtually every policy issue

(Gershman, 1975). Among the unions that showed an active interest in the conflict were several with large Jewish constituencies such as the Retail, Wholesale, and Department Store Union, and the International Ladies Garment Workers Union. But other large unions, such as the Teamsters and the National Maritime Union, were also active supporters of Israel. American labor was the most consistent opinion group in terms of policy stances, with almost all observable activities expended on displays of support for Israel, and attacks on the policies of the Arab states, the United States, the P.L.O., and the United Nations. The labor movement's size, its ability to mobilize, and its independent access to American policy-makers offsets its relatively low level of publicly recorded activities and belies its importance as a domestic ally of the pro-Israel movement.

The voice of the anti-Zionist segment of the articulate public was barely audible in the debates surrounding the Arab-Israeli conflict. As previously mentioned, internal problems within the movement during and after the June War wreaked organizational havoc. As a result, the forces of anti-Zionism have been for all practical purposes mute since 1968. Over the entire nine-year period, anti-Zionist groups concentrated their limited efforts on attacking pro-Israel initiatives, criticizing what they saw as the pro-Israel bias in American foreign policy, and occasionally challenging both the motives and tactics of pro-Arab groups.

Implicit throughout virtually all of the interest group literature, and explicit in our conceptual framework, is the notion that there is a positive relationship between the level of an interest group's activity and its ability to affect policy outputs (see Holtzman, 1966; La Palombara, 1964; Key, 1961). To have a direct, observable effect on policy it is assumed that a group must first articulate its policy preferences to external audiences. The logic is that the more active a group is in expressing its policy position, the better its chances are of gaining consideration for its position from other members of the articulate public, the mass public, and most importantly, from policy-makers. In turn, the more consideration given to a group's policy position by decision-makers, the more likely the group is to affect the outputs that emerge from the policy-making process. Table 5 clearly shows that pro-Israel groups dominated public activity. In terms of sheer level of activity, we would expect pro-Israel groups to have had a significantly better chance of affecting decisional outputs than any other domestic opinion group. Whether or not pro-Israel groups capitalized on this advantage, however, remains an open question that cannot be answered through the crude measures provided by events data alone. In order to address the question seriously we must combine our quantitative descriptive analysis with a more qualitative approach and examine the awareness and receptivity of relevant policy-makers to interest group inputs, and then make assessments concerning the importance of this set of inputs relative to all others.

Events data can, however, provide one more set of clues that can help us to generate expectations about the potential ability of different groups to have a significant policy impact. In addition to a relatively high level of political activity, another frequently mentioned prerequisite to the exercise of influence is the ability to gain direct access to decision-makers (Gable 1958; Truman, 1971; Key, 1961; Eldersveld, 1958; Sayre and Kaufman, 1965). Direct interest group-government actor interaction is the mechanism by which a group can condense all its activities in the domestic environment into specific demands or preferences to be considered by decision-makers during the policy process. While there are many factors that ultimately determine a group's ability to gain access, such as the structure of the government, the nature of the issue, and policy-makers' perceptions of the legitimacy of the group's cause, these factors will come into play only when the group actively seeks direct access to governmental officials.

The data in Table 6 can be used to characterize the degree to which different segments of the articulate public sought direct access to government officials through their public activities, and to distinguish among opinion groups that appeared to use a more direct strategy versus a more indirect strategy for affecting policy outputs. We will recall from section I that a direct strategy relies on expressions of interest group policy preferences targeted at specific policy-makers, with the purpose of gaining consideration and support from these government officials. An indirect strategy relies on other nongovernmental actors and elements (such as public opinion polls) in the domestic political environment in order to transmit the policy preferences of the group to policy-makers.

It is assumed in events data research that every act represents an attempt by the initiator (actor) to influence some identifiable individual, group, or other political entity. Those who theoretically receive and react to (and are therefore potentially influenced by) the messages conveyed by the actions are the "targets" of the actions. "Direct targets" are those that are specifically mentioned by the actors. Some direct targets are much more specific than others, and some are more relevant to the policy-making process than others. Table 6 lists some of the most frequently mentioned direct targets of interest group activity during the 1966-1974 period, and shows how the most active opinion groups distributed their publicly recorded activities in terms of these targets. The first thing that is evident about the targets listed in Table 6 is how non-specific *all* the targets appear to be. Two points are relevant here. First, most domestic interest groups were often very vague concerning exactly who should respond to their actions. Simply put, many events had no identifiable target. In such cases, the PANGA coding convention was to assume that the American mass public was, by default, the "target." Second, for the purposes of this table, a number of more specific targets have been grouped together under more general headings. The result is that some of the

TABLE 6
Opinion Group Activity by Selected Targets, 1966-1974

OPINION GROUP		President	U.S. Govt.	Congress	U.N.	Public	U.S. Jews	U.S. Christians	Corporations	Arab-Americans	Subtotals	Other	Total
Pro-Israel	N Row % Col %	75 10.0- 72.1	153 20.4 61.0	16 2.1 70.0	69 9.2 67.0	137 18.3 51.7	55 7.3 71.4	9 1.2 64.3	5 0.7 50.0	11 1.5 84.6	530 70.7	220 29.3	750 100
Pro-Arab	N Row % Col %	13 8.0 12.5	23 14.2 9.2	3 1.8 13.0	16 9.9 16.0	47 29.0 17.7	8 4.9 10.4	0 0.0 0.0	0 0.0 0.0	0 0.0 0.0	110 67.8	52 32.2	162 100
Church-Neutral	N Row % Col %	0 0.0 0.0	25 25.8 10.0	0 0.0 0.0	10 10.3 10.0	26 26.8 9.8	2 2.1 2.6	4 4.1 28.6	0 0.0 0.0	0 0.0 0.0	67 69.1	30 30.9	97 100
Business	N Row % Col %	4 7.5 3.8	8 15.1 3.2	0 0.0 0.0	3 5.7 2.9	19 35.8 7.2	2 3.8 2.6	1 1.9 7.1	4 7.5 40.0	0 0.0 0.0	41 77.3	12 22.7	53 100
Professional/ Educational	N Row % Col %	6 12.5 5.8	14 29.2 5.6	3 6.3 13.0	2 4.2 2.0	11 22.9 4.2	0 0.0 0.0	0 0.0 0.0	1 2.1 10.0	1 2.1 7.7	38 79.3	10 20.7	48 100
Blacks	N Row % Col %	0 0.0 0.0	7 15.2 2.8	0 0.0 0.0	0 0.0 0.0	9 19.6 3.4	3 6.5 3.9	0 0.0 0.0	0 0.0 0.0	1 2.2 7.7	20 43.5	35 56.5	46 100
Other Opinion Groups	N Row % Col %	6 7.4 5.8	21 25.9 8.4	1 1.2 4.0	3 3.7 2.9	16 19.8 6.1	7 8.6 9.1	0 0.0 0.0	0 0.0 0.0	0 0.0 0.0	54 66.6	27 33.3	81 99.9*
Column N		104	251	23	103	265	77	14	10	13			
Column %		100%	100.2%*	100%	100.3%*	100.1%*	100%	100%	100%	100%			

*Due to Rounding Error.

events directed at the broad targets in Table 6 were actually directed toward more specific, identifiable individuals or organizations.

In analyzing Table 6 we must recognize both that there is probably considerable slippage between the conceptual notions of access and targeting strategies and the empirical indicators used here, and that there is no reason to assume that a more direct strategy *necessarily* leads to greater policy impact. However, even with these qualifications, it can still be defensibly argued that the more an opinion group channels its policy preferences directly to governmental decision-makers rather than to other targets in the domestic or international environment, the more likely it is to have an identifiable impact on policy. And as crude as the target headings are, they do distinguish between targets that are, by definition, more likely to be primary or secondary participants in the policy formulation process—Congress, the president, and the U.S. government—and other targets residing in the domestic and international environments that have no formal policy-making authority.

The apparent targeting strategies of various opinion groups can be determined by comparing how all the actions initiated by each group are distributed among the alternative targets listed in Table 6. A comparison of the row percentages (middle figure in each cell) provides this information and yields interesting findings. First, all the opinion groups appeared to follow a targeting strategy that was heavily weighted in favor of the more indirect approach to affecting policy. Summing the percentage of each group's total activity directed toward all the governmental targets listed shows that none of the opinion groups directed even one-half of its public activities toward policy-makers. Most opinion groups selected governmental officials as primary targets for 30 percent or less of their public actions. When we take into account that a large proportion of the actions directed at "the government" failed to specify any particular individual or organization within the government, estimates of the relative frequency of direct interest group-to-policy-maker interaction must be revised downward even further. Thus, it appears that all the major opinion groups devoted considerably more effort to expressing their policy preferences toward other nongovernmental groups and the public at large than they did toward the governmental actors formally responsible for making American Middle East policy. The implication is that if any opinion group has had a significant impact on policy, its effects are likely to have been mediated through other actors or elements in the domestic environment.

Second, the most direct strategy was employed by professional and educational groups which targeted the greatest relative percentage of total activities toward policy-makers, with pro-Israel groups ranking second. Black groups employed what appeared to be the most indirect strategy, directing the lowest percentage of total actions toward government officials. Business, pro-Arab, and church and neutral groups were in the middle range, each targeting roughly a quarter of their actions at policy-makers. These differences in targeting strategies take on greater significance when coupled with differences in the levels of activity. We would expect that a relatively more direct (or less indirect) strategy would yield a significant advantage only if it resulted in the group gaining relatively more frequent access to decision-makers than other groups. Table 6 shows that while in relative terms professional and educational groups targeted more of their actions toward policy-makers than any other groups, in *absolute* terms pro-Israel groups dominated the flow of public activities into the government. The bottom figure in each cell (column %) represents the percentage of all events directed toward a given target by a given opinion group. It can be seen that pro-Israel groups accounted for 70 percent of all actions targeted at Congress, 72 percent of all those aimed directly at the president and 61 percent of all activities targeted at the U.S. government, its agencies, and individuals within the government. Moreover, pro-Israel groups also dominated the stream of actions directed toward each of the other listed targets in the domestic and international environments. Thus, on the basis of both targeting strategy and volume it appears that pro-Israel groups were the primary sources of domestic inputs on Middle East issues during the 1966-1974 period. As a result we would expect pro-Israel groups to have had a decided advantage over their domestic competitors in their potential ability to affect the substance of American policy toward the Arab-Israeli conflict.

Conclusions

Although the macro-, micro-, and middle level perspectives range considerably in terms of units of analysis, each has contributed to a set of behavioral characteristics that appears to be closely related to the ability of interest groups to exercise influence. Combining conceptual arguments from all three perspectives, we have argued that the potential for observable interest group impact in a given policy decision is likely to be relatively great when:

(1) manifest public interest is relatively intense and is sustained over the course of the policy debate;
(2) the debates initiated and led by interest groups focus on identifiable policy problems;
(3) a reasonably clear policy consensus in support of a given policy position or party to the conflict emerges from the public debates; and
(4) the policy preferences of interest groups are transmitted directly to relevant policy-makers.

Given these behavioral prerequisites for policy impact, empirical findings have been used to generate some expectations about the likely ability of domestic groups to affect American Middle East policy. These expectations fall into two categories. The first set concerns the potential policy impact of the articulate public taken as an undifferentiated whole. In general, we expect the policy impact of all domestic groups to be relatively weak to the extent that:

(1) public interest in most Middle East issues has been sporadic, with sharp increases in attention coming largely only during periods of military crisis and as reactions to policies already formulated and implemented;

(2) groups tend to concentrate considerably more attention on general, nonsubstantive issues than on more narrow, identifiable policy issues;

(3) while general support for Israel has been strong, this consensus tends to break down on many specific policy issues, with the result that non-governmental inputs on many issues frequently either are "mixed," with no apparent consensus, or run contrary to the prevailing trends of sentiment; and

(4) groups tend to direct their policy preferences considerably more often toward other actors in the domestic environment than toward the government officials formally responsible for making policy.

While recognizing these general constraints, the second set of expectations concerns the *relative* potential of different segments of the articulate public to see their policy preferences translated into decisional outputs. Empirical results from all three analytic perspectives consistently show that relative to all other opinion groups in the domestic environment pro-Israel groups are most likely to exert an impact on policy because:

(1) pro-Israel groups have succeeded in generating and maintaining widespread general support for Israel from most other actors among the articulate public, and have largely succeeded in intimidating or isolating those groups least likely to support a pro-Israel policy stance;

(2) they are the most numerous and the most active set of domestic groups on most issues; and

(3) they have dominated the flow of policy demands from the domestic environment into the governmental policy-making arena.

The behavioral characteristics discussed above represent some of the independent variables that can be operationalized to help explain variations in the policy impact of interest groups. Other important behavioral variables that have not been considered here, such as whether an expression of policy preference comes before or after a decision has been made, must be properly operationalized before we can derive a behavioral "model" that seeks to explain when and how interest groups affect foreign policy. However, we should probably be much less worried about the independent variable side of the equation than about the dependent variable side. All the expectations generated from exploratory behavioral analyses such as this will necessarily remain untested until we find a viable operational measure for the dependent variable, policy impact. This is likely to be a difficult if not impossible task given current soical science methods. Despite these important problems, there do exist ways of tapping not only public, "countable" domestic group behavior but also the more discrete, unpublicized activities and relationships that help determine the impact—however defined—of any interest group.

PRO-ISRAEL AND PRO-ARAB INTEREST GROUPS: A COMPARATIVE ANALYSIS

Thus far in our empirical investigation we have identified the wide range of domestic groups that took an interest in the Arab-Israeli conflict. We have examined various dimensions of their public behavior and made some tentative judgments concerning the likely ability of different sets of groups to affect governmental policy. However, we have not yet grappled with the broader and more difficult problem of explaining why selected groups behaved as they did during the 1966-1974 period, nor have we examined some of the other important variables that helped determine the policy-making roles assumed by different groups. In this section we shall conduct a comparative analysis of the two most publicly active opinion groups, and those with the greatest direct interest in the Arab-Israeli conflict and American Middle East policy. These groups are domestic pro-Israel and pro-Arab interest groups. We will want to examine some of the effects of organizational characteristics, the structure of the decision-making system, and relationships with other actors in the domestic environment on the behavior and potential impact of these two movements. We shall use the arguments and propositions developed in section I as our frame of reference in interpreting the results, which are based on interviews with interest group leaders and policy-makers as well as empirical data.

Organizational Characteristics

In their classic study of the making of American foreign trade legislation, Bauer, Pool, and Dexter (1963: 324) conclude that the organizational weaknesses of most interest groups limited their ability to play meaningful policy-making roles:

> It ... came as a surprise to discover that the lobbies were on the whole poorly financed, ill-managed, out of contact with Congress, and at best marginally effective in supporting tendencies and measures which already had behind them considerably congressional impetus from other sources.... When we look at a typical lobby, we find that its opportunities for maneuver are sharply limited, its staff mediocre and its major problem not the influencing of Congressional votes but the finding of clients and contributions to enable it to survive at all.

While it is difficult to know what a "typical" interest group is, the above description is a much better characterization of a number of pro-Arab and anti-Zionist groups than it is of most pro-Israel groups. Organizations such as the Action Committee on American Arab Relations, Americans for Justice in the Middle East, and American Jewish Alternatives to Zionism are essentially "one-man shows," run on a financial shoestring, with relatively small memberships that rely almost totally on periodic newsletters for information from their leaders. The facts that there are no more than 500,000 Arab-

Americans in the entire United States, that the occasional "radical" tone of their rhetoric inhibits a lot of sympathizers from formally identifying with pro-Arab groups, and that many of the pro-Arab leaders have deemphasized the need for strong bureaucracies, can in large part account for the weak state of their organizational structures. There is little doubt that the absence of any mass membership pro-Arab groups until the formation of the National Association of Arab Americans in 1972 created severe handicaps for the pro-Arab movement in this country, both in terms of financial capabilities and the abilities of a small core of dedicated but overworked pro-Arab leaders to compete effectively with their pro-Israel counterparts.

While Bauer, Pool, and Dexter's characterization may also be applicable to some of the smaller, more radical pro-Israel groups, such as the Jewish Defense League or Hashomir Hatzair, it does not fit the bulk of American Jewish groups. On the contrary, most major Jewish groups are characterized by large memberships, well-trained professional staffs, adequately financed social, welfare, and political programs, specialized working groups for particular problems, and elaborate internal communications networks. For example, Hadassah, the Women's Zionist Organization of America, is the largest women's organization in the country, with 325,000 members distributed over 1,400 local chapters. It is run by a national board of approximately 140 people that convenes twice a year to consider major policy positions. Minor policy decisions are made and distributed to local units on a weekly basis by an executive board in New York. The Zionist Organization of America (ZOA), with a membership of around 45,000, has 500 local districts and 20 professionally-staffed regional offices spread across the 50 states. There are 265 local representatives on the national executive committee of ZOA, plus a professional staff of 12 for the national office, which administers an average budget of $1.6 million for summer youth programs, a cultural center in Jerusalem, welfare programs, and other projects, in addition to its foreign policy activities. The examples could go on and on: The Jewish War Veterans of the U.S.A.—600 local posts and 100,000 members; the American Jewish Congress—40,000 members; the National Council of Jewish Women—100,000 members.

More important than just the numbers, however, are the bureaucratic machines that have been built by these organizations and that tie politically active Jews throughout the country to centralized leadership groups such as the Presidents Conference and AIPAC, facilitating communication flows between pro-Israel opinion leaders and their publics. Jews are the most urbanized ethnic group in America, with 66 percent living in communities of one million people or more (Gallup and Davies, 1971: 57). They also show the highest rate of membership in voluntary organizations of any religious group in the country (Wright and Hyman, 1958: 287). These factors, when combined with the numerous organizational communications channels linking national elites to regional, state, and local leaders, give Jewish groups the potential ability to respond much more quickly and in much larger numbers than pro-Arab groups.

The multitiered structural pyramid that links individual Jews in local communities across the country to centralized national foreign policy leadership groups in Washington and New York is the primary organizational factor that can explain the ability of the pro-Israel movement to mobilize rapidly and in a coordinated fashion on a national scale when important foreign policy issues arise. At the community level, individuals belong to local units of national organizations or to local community relations organizations. As previously noted, local branches may be tied to their national leaders through district or regional offices as well as directly through the national office. Most national organizations belong to umbrella groups that bring together local and national groups operating in related areas: religious affairs (Synagogue Council of America); community relations (National Jewish Community Relations Advisory Council); labor (National Council for Labor Israel); Zionist affairs (American Zionist Federation); youth affairs (North American Jewish Youth Council) and so on. Finally, these functionally specific umbrella groups belong to the Conference of Presidents of Major American Jewish Organizations or are affiliated with the American Israel Public Affairs Committee, the only two domestic pro-Israel groups that are tax-paying, registered domestic lobbies. The Presidents Conference and AIPAC are responsible for funneling the policy preferences agreed upon by the representatives of organized American Jewry to decision-makers in the executive and congressional branches of government and to foreign leaders. They also provide information, guidance, and coordination for the political activities of the leaders of national organizations, who, in turn, send political directives and advice down the organizational ladder to regional, district, and local leaders, who spread the word to individual members.

A comparison of the organizational characteristics of the pro-Arab and pro-Israel movements supports Holtzman's (1966: 33) contention that

> Failure to create an association of groups may result in a babble of voices being heard, none of which is really concerned with the interests of the others in the more inclusive group of which they are members. Even if common goals or actions are agreed upon, without a broader organization to integrate and implement decisions, inaction or confusion is often the inevitable consequence.[8]

Such problems consistently plagued the pro-Arab movement during the period under discussion, and inhibited its ability to compete effectively with the pro-Israel movement. Many of the difficulties of the pro-Arab movement can be attributed to the lack of consensus on basic political and tactical issues among the movement's leaders on the one hand, and between the leaders and their followers on the other. The leaders of the most politically active pro-Arab groups are generally foreign born, naturalized Americans. However, owing to the relatively small Arab-American population in the United States, their main body of potential support resides with pro-Arab, native-born Americans. Serious splits have developed over time between the foreign-born and the native-born in the pro-Arab movement, despite the fact that both sets of leaders share a common commitment to advancing the pro-Arab cause in this country. The inability of the two groups to resolve their differences has led to serious problems of coordination and a "babble of voices" within the pro-Arab movement.

In interviews American-born pro-Arab leaders described their Middle Eastern-born counterparts as "domineering," "obstinate," and "self-serving." The major complaint of the native-born was that the foreign-born had no grasp of American politics, and refused to take advice on how to better the public image of the pro-Arab movement and how to present their policy positions to decision-makers in an effective manner. The result, contended the American-born, was that the anti-Zionist rhetoric, the street demonstrations, and the disregard shown the mass media by groups such as ACAAR and the Organization of Arab Students served only to alienate the American public and the policy-makers they were seeking to win over. Furthermore, some American-born Arab supporters are corporate executives who favor a quieter and more direct approach to decision-makers that is more in keeping with the political style of corporations in general. These differences have prevented the formation of coalitions not only within the pro-Arab movement, but also between pro-Arab groups and some corporate groups with economic holdings in the Middle East that share some of the same policy objectives. We will discuss pro-Arab group-corporate relations in more detail when we consider how interest groups interact with other elements in the domestic environment. We should recognize, however, that one reason pro-Arab groups could not compete on the same scale with pro-Israel groups was their inability and unwillingness to match the organizational strength of the pro-Israel movement.

Structure of the Decision-Making System

In section I the argument was made that for each policy issue there are routinized procedures that define some minimum number of governmental actors—the "core" actors—who normally carry primary responsibility for handling problems in that area. In addition there are "secondary" governmental actors who seek a role in the process because of personal or organizational interest in the issue. For interest groups to affect policy they must not only gain access to governmental actors who are sympathetic to their policy preferences, but they must get support from governmental actors who can, themselves, make a meaningful input into the decision that finally emerges. As the efficacy of different governmental actors to which interest groups have access varies from issue to issue, so will the potential influence of nongovernmental groups.

While there are many specific issues that make up the "Arab-Israeli conflict," it is possible to cluster a number of issues under one or another of the two broad headings: "American peace-making policy" and "American arms sales policy." Peace-making policy refers to active attempts by the United States to resolve the conflict in the Middle East. Examples of specific American peace initiatives include President Johnson's "Five Great Principles Speech," of June 1967; the "Rogers Plan" of December 1969; the American cease-fire initiative of July 1970 (sometimes called Rogers Plan II); the Egyptian-Israeli and Syrian-Israeli troop disengagement agreements of 1974; and the Sinai Agreement of 1975. Arms sales policy refers to cash sales, credit sales, and grants of military equipment by the United States to Israel and the Arab governments. Some of the largest arms transfer during the 1966-1974 period were the sale of F-4 (Phantom) fighter-bombers to Israel in 1968, 1970, and 1971, and the massive $2.2 billion grant to Israel for the resupply of arms after the 1973 war. There is a general consensus among political analysts that pro-Israel interest groups were much more effective in influencing arms sales decisions than they were in influencing the substance of American peace initiatives.[9] There is also a consensus that pro-Arab groups had a negligible impact on both sets of issues. Although peace-making and arms sales issues were often closely related, there were differences in policy-making structure between the two clusters that had significant effects on the potential impact of the pro-Arab and pro-Israel groups.

The major difference in the two policy-making systems was the larger number of governmental actors that could legitimately claim and exert a primary role in the determination of arms sales policies (such as DOD, CIA, and Congress) relative to the constricted circle of decision-makers (State, the president, and NSC) responsible for formulating American peace initiatives. Of particular importance were the different roles played by Congress on the two sets of issues. Pro-Israel groups enjoyed direct access and unwavering support from a substantial majority of the members of Congress for their policy stands on both peace and arms sales issues.[10] However, congressional support on diplomatic questions resulted in negligible payoffs for pro-Israel groups because Congress had no claim to direct participation in the development of peace initiatives, and because State Department officials—who *were* primarily responsible for policy formulation—were generally as unreceptive to congressional forays into the process as they were to interest group inputs.

The situation was quite different, however, for the process dealing with arms sales. In this case, Congress enjoyed equal status with State as a core actor, owing to its control over military and economic aid appropriations. It used its power to Israel's advantage in 1968, 1970, and 1971 by appropriating the arms sales credits necessary to buy F-4's before the president had even made the decision to sell the jets. And, after the October War of 1973, Congress added a half billion dollars to the administration's request for supplemental military assistance to Israel. Although in all cases ultimate decisional power resided with the president, pro-Israel groups were able to use their close ties with Congress to help spur the president toward a favorable decision.

Congress's willingness to support pro-Israel positions is the product of a number of complex factors, with determinants varying in importance for individual congressmen. For some, responsiveness to constituents' demands and reliance on campaign contributions from Jewish backers have probably been the primary considerations (Rudeneh, 1972). For others, a personal sense of identification with Israel and the Israelis, or a view of Israel as a bastion of democracy that must be kept strong to prevent Soviet domination of the area, have led them to be receptive to requests for support from pro-Israel groups. Overlaying these more specific elements is the general factor that for whatever reasons a particular congressman supports Israel, he is likely to be well in the mainstream of articulate opinion in his home district or state. For many Americans, congressional backing for Israel has come to be generally expected, irrespective of the ethnic or religious make-up of the district. The pro-Israel sentiments of the mass media and major non-Jewish segments of the articulate public—which includes many congressmen as private individuals—may be at least as important in determining congressional reactions as the electoral strength and the direct lobbying efforts of pro-Israel groups.

The relationship between congressional behavior and other elements in the domestic environment is circular. Congressional support is important because of its legitimizing and sanctioning effects for the activities of interest groups, and the more or less direct access to the media and to core governmental actors enjoyed by congressmen. An unreceptive Congress creates severe handicaps for a nongovernmental actor. If a group is forced to rely solely on its own political resources, it will rarely be able to marshal the support from the mass and articulate publics necessary to play an effective policy-making role. But, of course, the ability to petition Congress for support with success appears to be closely tied to an ability to get widespread support from the articulate public. One generally does not come without the other. As is the case with other relevant domestic actors, interest groups are dependent on Congress for amplifying and disseminating their policy preferences in a manner that is beyond their own capabilities. If Congress fails to provide these services, the nongovernmental actor is likely to find itself isolated, as many pro-Arab groups did, in a political environment that is generally unaware or unsupportive of its policy objectives.

The notable lack of success of both pro-Israel and pro-Arab groups in affecting the substance of American peace initiatives can be attributed largely to the generally cool receptions given to their demands by the State Department and the White House. Both sets of governmental targets, but particularly those in the State Department, were unable to agree with the arguments of domestic groups that they had a legitimate right to participate actively in the formulation of policy. I do not subscribe to the idea (Kraft, 1971) that pro-Israel groups generally did not get along with State Department officials because State was filled with "Arabists" who "favored" the Arabs over Israel in the conflict. If anything, State Department people were at least as unreceptive to pro-Arab group demands as they were to those made by pro-Israel groups.

The reasons for the inability of both pro-Israel and pro-Arab groups to gain support from the State Department were more closely tied to the perceptions of officials throughout the department as to what their policy-making roles and responsibilities were and what the "proper" role of domestic groups should be, than to the cultural (or political) affinities of a small group of individuals. A recurring theme in interviews with State Department personnel was the importance they placed on being able to formulate American foreign policy on the basis of broad "national interests," unfettered by the partisan political interests of domestic governmental and nongovernmental actors. Demands from Congress as well as interest groups were generally viewed as motivated by narrow interests that were not necessarily compatible with the broader interests that State sought to safeguard and advance. The results was that most domestic foreign policy activities were seen as unwarranted intrusions into a decision-making arena that should be reserved for professionals with a better conception of "America's" foreign political and strategic objectives.[11] State's persistent struggle to remain aloof from domestic political debates and to preserve its national perspective toward international politics, in large part explains its general unwillingness to bestow legitimacy on interest group activities.

The behavior of pro-Israel and pro-Arab groups during the 1966-1974 period supports the proposition that groups prefer to target their demands at "friendly" targets who are predisposed to support their policy positions. Pro-Israel groups interacted directly with the State Department much less than they did with Congress because they believed that support was much easier to extract from Congress, even though on most diplomatic issues Congress was not a primary governmental actor. When pro-Israel groups did direct their efforts at State, they tended to be highly selective in their choice of targets, preferring to talk with officials previously identified as supportive of pro-Israel positions.

Pro-Arab groups generally believed the entire governmental structure to be unsympathetic to their policy positions, and only rarely interacted directly with any governmental actors. In interviews, pro-Arab leaders expressed the view that there were few differences in the receptivity of various individuals or agencies within the government. Congress, the State Department, and the White House were all perceived by pro-Arab groups to be the captives of the pro-Israel lobby. Consequently, pro-Arab groups expended little effort on what they believed would be futile attempts to win the support of policy-makers through direct communication. The result was that pro-Arab groups consistently remained on the periphery of the decision-making process, doomed by their lack of direct interaction with decision-makers to have a negligible impact on policy outputs.

The Domestic Environment

The advantage enjoyed by pro-Israel groups over pro-Arab groups in gaining support from other actors in the domestic environment was even more pronounced than the relative success of their direct influence-seeking efforts. An examination of the relationships between pro-Israel and pro-Arab groups on the one hand, and mass public opinion, the mass media, and other relevant opinion groups on the other, will dispel some common misunderstandings and will carry us far toward explaining the differences in behavior and potential impact of the two movements.

Mass Public Opinion: In section I the argument was made that mass public opinion can have an impact on the policy-making process in at least two ways, both of which carry implications for the success of indirect interest group efforts. First, public opinion can affect the behavior of decision-makers by providing clear indications of public support (or lack of it) for specific policy proposals. Interest groups are likely to increase their indirect influence to the extent that they can rally public opinion behind proposals that reflect their policy preferences. Neither pro-Israel nor pro-Arab interest groups were able to generate or maintain mass public support for any specific solution to the Arab-Israeli conflict during the 1967 through 1975 period. This lack of success can be explained in part by the fact that pro-Israel and pro-Arab groups often did not have *specific* solutions to propose. What appears to be an even more important factor, however, is that the bulk of the American populace became increasingly supportive of either a "hands off" or a "neutral mediator" American policy toward the conflict during the 1967-1975 period, alternatives advocated by neither the pro-Israel nor pro-Arab movements. Table 7 presents Gallup poll data on the opinions of nationwide samples of people concerning what the United States should do about the Middle East.[12] The data in Table 7 are self-explanatory. In each of the five samples, a sizable majority of the respondents either had no opinion or thought that the wisest course of action for the United States government was to stay clear of the conflict.

Although pro-Israel groups worked even harder for American economic and military arms support for Israel (but never for American troops) after

TABLE 7
American Public Opinion on Alternative U.S. Policies Toward the Arab-Israeli Conflict (Based on Informed Group)

Question:	What Should U.S. do About Situation?	What Should U.S. do in Event of War?	What Should U.S. do About Situation?	What Should U.S. do About Situation?	What do you Think the U.S. Should do in This Situation?
Date:	June 1967	July 1968	February 1969	February 1970	April 1975
Solution:					
1. Stay out of Conflict	41%	61%	52%	58%	41%
2. Support Israel (Non-Military Aid)	16	10	13	13	5
3. Negotiate for Peace/ Act as Mediator	14	8	11	10	24
4. Work Through U.N./ Reconvene Geneva Convention	11	3	2	2	1
5. Support Israel (Send Troops)	5	*	1	1	*
6. Support Arab States	*	*	1	1	*
7. No opinion, Other	13	20	20	15	31
Totals	100%	102%**	100%	100%	102%**

*Less than 1/2%.
**Adds to more than 100% because of multiple responses.

the June War and the October War, the support of the informed public for this policy alternative declined slightly after the summer of 1967, stabilizing at around 13 percent in favor of aid in 1969 and 1970, and slipping to 5 percent in favor by spring 1975. The tendency of the mass public to favor noninvolvement increased noticeably when the question arose as to how the government should respond to a hypothetical war situation. However, given the American experience in Vietnam it is not surprising that in July 1968, a majority of the American public was reluctant to commit troops to the Middle East. While public support for a governmental policy favoring the Arab states was negligible, the support that pro-Israel groups were able to generate for any specifically pro-Israel American policy was not commensurate with their efforts.

Since government officials have been committed to an active peace-making policy since the June War (see Quandt, 1972, 1974; Safran, 1969, 1974; Ullman, 1975; Spiegel, 1973), and have therefore in effect been ignoring the preferences of the largest opinion cluster within the mass public, the scattered support for other specific alternatives could not be viewed as a serious constraint on their freedom of action. The increase in public support for governmental efforts to mediate the dispute carries implications concerning the relative abilities of interest groups and the government to rally public opinion behind specific courses of action. Secretary of State Kissinger's "step-by-step" diplomacy following the 1973 war, which led to the Egyptian-Israeli and Syrian-Israeli disengagement agreements and the Sinai Agreement of 1975, was consistently and loudly opposed by leading groups within the American pro-Israel movement.[13] Yet by April 1975, public support for a mediating role for the United States government was greater than for any other sample during the nine year period.

A second way that mass public opinion can affect the policy impact of interest groups is by becoming a relevant part of the "cultural milieu" that helps shape the perceptions and behavior of governmental policy-makers. Interest groups that are able to frame their arguments in terms of general, long-standing "national traditions" hold an advantage to the extent that policy momentum favors their preferences, and that they are more likely to elicit automatic support from both decision-makers and the mass public.

The general belief among most journalists is that the American people have always been "overwhelmingly" sympathetic toward Israel's position in the dispute.[14] Table 8 shows this finding to be warranted, but only when the data are considered in relative rather than absolute terms. A Gallup poll taken in November 1947 found that in the event of war, 24 percent of the American public would sympathize with the Jews, 12 percent with the Arabs, 38 percent would favor neither party, and 26 percent had no opinion (Erskine, 1970: 629). When war broke out in the winter of 1947-1948, American support for both sides—but particularly for Israel—increased, with 35 percent favoring the Jews, 16 percent supporting the Arabs, and 49 percent sympathizing with neither side or having no opinion. It is certainly the case that informed Americans have consistently been much more willing to declare general support for Israel than for the Arab states. No more than 8 percent of the mass public ever expressed sympathy for the Arab states during the 1967-1975 period, while up to 60 percent expressed support for Israel. However, Table 8 also shows that general public sympathy for Israel has tended to decline since the June War. The two exceptions to this trend followed the discovery of Soviet-Egyptian violations of the 1970 cease-fire agreements and the declaration of the Arab oil embargo shortly after the October War. By May 1975, however, the level of mass public support for Israel had slipped to the point (37 percent) where it was only two percentage points higher than during the struggle for Israeli independence in the winter of 1947-1948.

The pattern in recent years has been for an increasing percentage of the mass public to favor neither side in the conflict and to refuse to take a position. In absolute terms, Table 8 shows that pro-Israel groups lost ground despite their persistent and extensive efforts to maintain at least a majority of the American public openly sympathetic to Israel's cause. However, the data also show that pro-Arab groups have had to operate in a domestic environment that provides little, if any, mass support. And in relative terms, pro-Israel groups have consistently maintained a wide lead over their pro-

TABLE 8
American Public Opinion Toward the Parties to the Arab-Israeli Conflict

Question: In This Trouble, are Your Sympathies More With Israel or More With the Arab States?*

Date:	June 1967	Feb. 1969	Feb. 1970	July 1970	Aug. 1970 (Harris)	Oct. 1970 (Harris)	Oct. 1973	Dec. 1973	Jan. 1975	May 1975
Preference:										
Israel	56%	50%	44%	60%	47%	47%	48%	54%	44%	37%
Arab States	4	5	3	8	6	6	6	8	8	8
Neither	25	28	32	8	25	26	21	24	22	24
No Opinion	15	17	21	24	22	21	25	14	26	31
Totals	100%	100%	100%	100%	100%	100%	100%	100%	100%	100%

*All data are from the Gallup Opinion Index except for August 1970 and October 1970, which are responses to the same question asked by the Harris poll.

Arab competitors in the contest for the sympathies of the American mass public.

Mass Media: Pro-Israel groups were much more successful in building and maintaining strong support for Israel from syndicated American columnists than they were in their efforts to mold mass public opinion. One of the most serious political handicaps of pro-Arab groups during the 1966-1974 period was their inability to gain support from any of the best known and nationally-syndicated political columnists. We can get an idea of the relative advantage enjoyed by pro-Israel groups among these key influentials by reviewing the findings of an analysis made of the columns published by 18 writers with Washington outlets over a 17 day period running from May 28 through June 13, 1967 (American Institute for Political Communication, 1967). Each of the columns surveyed appeared in roughly 100 newspapers on the average, with the exception of those of Drew Pearson and Jack Anderson, which appeared in more than 600 papers.

The 18 writers published 58 different columns during the period leading up to and including the June War. Only five of the columnists wrote only one piece on the conflict: Howard K. Smith, Clayton Fritchey, and Charles Bartlett tended to view the crisis primarily as an American foreign policy problem, while Max Lerner and Ralph McGill took a strong, pro-Israel position. Table 9 lists the 13 Washington writers who published two or more columns, their Washington newspaper outlet, the number of columns each published, and their general political orientation toward the crisis. A columnist was viewed as "pro-Israeli" if he generally adhered to a position consistent with the aims or policies of the Israeli government, "pro-Arab" if he generally supported the aims or policies of the Arab states, "U.S. policy-oriented" if his position was generally consistent with expressed American policy, and "neutral" if he took no substantive position on the Middle East crisis.

Six columnists consistently took a pro-Israeli position, accounting for about 20 of the 58 columns. None of the writers surveyed adopted a pro-Arab position, and Marquis Childs was the only columnist to publish a piece on the needs and problems of the Arabs, and the plight of the Palestinian refugees. May and June of 1967, of course, were not "normal" months, particularly because of the emotions raised by the intensity of the political and military activities leading up to the war and the war itself. However, this survey is representative of the general support that pro-Israel groups derived from a small but influential group of opinion leaders relative to pro-Arab groups, whose preferences were generally either ignored or rejected by the national columnists.

Pro-Israel groups could count on media support not only from a number of national columnists but also from the editors of some of the country's most widely read newspapers. The nonpartisan American Institute for Politi-

TABLE 9
The General Orientations of Thirteen Syndicated Columnists on the Middle East Crisis and War, May 28-June 13, 1967

Columnist	Washington Outlet	No. of Columns	Orientation
David Lawrence	The Star	8	U.S. Policy
Pearson-Anderson	The Post	7	Pro-Israeli
Joseph Alsop	The Post	5	Pro-Israeli
Evans-Novak	The Post	5	U.S. Policy
Joseph Kraft	The Post	5	Pro-Israeli
Richard Wilson	The Star	5	U.S. Policy
Marquis Childs	The Post	4	U.S. Policy
Carl Rowan	The Star	4	U.S. Policy
Doris Fleeson	The Star	3	U.S. Policy; Pro-Israeli
Crosby Noyes	The Star	3	U.S. Policy
John Chamberlain	The Post	2	Pro-Israeli
Rosco Drummund	The Post	2	U.S. Policy; Pro-Israeli
William White	The Post	2	Neutral

Source: American Institute for Political Communication.

cal Communication (1967) conducted a survey of 28 editorials in 10 major morning newspapers during the May 23-29, 1967 period, and concluded that there was general condemnation of the Egyptian blockade of the Gulf of Aqaba, general support for Israel, an emphasis on the use of the United Nations to solve the crisis, and a general reluctance to see American troops committed unilaterally to the conflict. These papers—*Atlanta Constitution, Chicago Tribune, Detroit Free Press, Houston Post, Los Angeles Times, New York Times, Philadelphia Inquirer, Seattle Post-Intelligencer, St. Louis Globe-Democrat,* and the *Washington Post*—represent 20 percent of the nation's total morning newspaper circulation, and 8 percent of total daily circulation. As such, they are a significant force in the molding of both mass and elite perceptions concerning the conflict. And while the national press tended to put limits on its support for certain kinds of U.S. aid to Israel (for example, no troops), the general predispositions of a number of American newspaper editors to support the Israeli cause made them active and important allies of pro-Israel interest groups.

Open support for Israel by syndicated columnists and editors of elite American newspapers represented an important advantage for pro-Israel groups. Equally important, however, may have been differences in the media's news coverage of the activities of pro-Israel and pro-Arab groups. While charges of media bias in reporting have never been confirmed, perceived discrimination in the coverage of pro-Arab statements and activities by the national press was one of the dominant themes that emerged from interviews with pro-Arab leaders. The only major newspaper exempted from this charge was the *Christian Science Monitor,* which was seen as providing equal coverage for all groups interested in the Middle East. Recognizing that most political advertisements and letters to the editor in major papers are ignored by policy-makers, some pro-Arab groups adopted a strategy of turning to smaller, local newspapers as the primary vehicles for distributing their side of the story. The rationale behind this indirect approach was that local papers are much more receptive than the national press, and that congressmen form their opinions on particular issues partly on the basis of the opinions carried in district newspapers. The idea was that if pro-Arab groups could win the support of local editors they might, in time, be able to turn the tide of congressional opinion, and thereby offset some of the liabilities created by the generally pro-Israel tone of the national press.

However, even on the local newspaper front, pro-Arab groups were outorganized and out-spent by pro-Israel groups. For example, in 1970 alone, the Mass Media Committee of the Presidents Conference prepared and distributed press relations kits containing feature stories on Israel, captioned photographs in mat form, and a supplementary service of additional features with photographs to 1,700 daily newspapers around the country. In addition, 1,000 newspapers with circulations under 5,000 were sent mat features (photos plus text) on Israel. These local-targeted activities supplemented the more routine efforts to have feature articles prepared by Conference staff members accepted by the national and international news services. The scorecard for 1970 included: 17 captioned photographs on life in Israel accepted by the Associated Press; 14 different photos selected by United Press International for distribution to clients; two feature stories and photographs included in *Parade Magazine* (a Sunday supplement with total circulation of more than 14 million); and assorted Israeli anniversary materials accepted by *Family Week*, Central Press, and the North American Newspaper Alliance (Conference of Presidents, 1971: 37-38). Thus, at virtually every level of media organization—from local communities, syndicated columnists, and major national papers, to the international news services that supply the country with information—pro-Israel groups were more successful than pro-Arab groups in getting their side of the story transmitted to both the articulate and mass publics. Although pro-Arab groups dramatically increased their media efforts after the October War, pro-Israel groups maintained a significant—if relatively smaller—advantage in garnering the support of the mass media for their policy preferences.

Intergroup Relations: If there is one factor that can best explain the more important foreign policy role played by pro-Israel groups relative to pro-Arab groups, it has been their differential abilities in forming coalitions with other domestic nongovernmental groups. The consistent ability of pro-Israel groups to enlist the support of significant numbers of non-Jewish groups has been one of the major determinants of Congress's receptivity to pro-Israel policy preferences. And if the pro-Israel movement has had any impact on foreign policy it has been as a result of the political support it has received from members of Congress. More important than the Jewish bloc vote and Jewish campaign contributions has been the capacity of pro-Israel groups to align themselves with more representative segments of the American population at the district and state levels.

We have previously discussed how pro-Israel groups used organizational devices such as umbrella groups to weld themselves into a cohesive movement on foreign policy issues. However, of equal importance are the linkages that bind Jewish individuals and groups laterally to non-Jewish individuals and groups in their domestic environment. No ethnic group, of course, need be characterized on ethnic or religious grounds alone. From a functional perspective, they can be lumped with members of other ethnic or religious groups to form different groups within the American population: businessmen, laborers, veterans, housewives, students, and so on. The degree to which pro-Israel groups are integrated into this broader, functionally-based network of groups and individuals permits them regularly to ask for and receive support from a large number of non-Jewish groups with similar functional identities and interests.

The relationships between the Jewish War Veterans of the U.S.A. (JWV) and other veterans organizations is a case in point. The JWV has a membership of approximately 100,000 veterans of foreign wars, who also happen to be Jewish. The membership of the JWV shares many of the same characteristics as the memberships of the American Legion and the Veteran of Foreign Wars (VFW). These three organizations work closely on the entire range of veterans affairs issues: hospital benefits, Veterans Administration housing loans, G.I. bill educational benefits, national security and foreign policy issues. Because of their common interests in veterans affairs, the Jewish War Veterans could and did approach the American Legion and the VFW for political support on issues of particular concern to the JWV, namely those related to the support of Israel in the Arab-Israeli conflict. The ability of the JWV to get the backing of other veterans groups on Middle East issues was a direct function of their similar interests and their cooperation on veterans and foreign policies issues other than the Middle East.

Another example of how pro-Israel groups can use their functional ties with other groups to political advantage can be found in the relationship between the National Council for Labor Israel and organized labor. The National Council is a member of the Presidents Conference, and is itself an umbrella group for Jewish labor organizations. The most politically active constituent member of the National Council is the Trade Union Council for Histadrut, which is also an independent member of the Presidents Conference. To make things more complex, the Trade Union Council is composed of leaders from the entire spectrum of American labor organizations, from conglomerate unions with predominantly non-Jewish memberships such as the AFL-CIO, to individual unions with large percentages of Jewish members such as the International Ladies Garment Workers Union and the Amalgamated Clothing Workers. This organizational web has integrated Jewish and non-Jewish labor interests and enabled groups such as the Trade Union Council and its parent organization, the National Council for Labor Israel, to rely on the support of a substantial portion of organized labor for their pro-Israel foreign policy positions. For example, George Meany, president of the A.F.L.-C.I.O. and one of the most outspoken supporters of Israel among American labor leaders, works closely with Jewish labor and is honorary chairman of the Trade Union Council. The result is that when the Trade Union Council takes a policy stand, it is not speaking solely for *Jewish* labor but rather for a significant proportion of *American* labor, whose influence extends far beyond that of the relatively small number of American Jewish workers.

The ability of pro-Israel groups to establish close working relationships with non-Jewish counterparts in the larger American society is one of the primary factors that permits them to disseminate their policy preferences far beyond their own organizational capabilities and to build the broad base of organized support that a pro-Israel American policy appears to have enjoyed among the articulate public. One reason that Jewish groups have been able to attain political leverage with non-Jewish groups is that in many areas, such as veterans affairs and labor, their absolute numbers are sufficiently large to give them an important say on matters of common, vital interest other than foreign policy. As a result of their close cooperation in these other areas, Jewish groups expect support for their pro-Israel policy positions. Arab-Americans, who number no more than about 500,000 and are more widely dispersed than the six million American Jews, can hardly be expected to compete effectively at the organizational level. One result is that pro-Arab groups have remained relatively isolated in the American domestic environment, unable to build and use lateral ties with larger segments of the articulate public to their political advantage.

Beyond the support they derive from functionally or politically related allies, nongovernmental groups also seek endorsements from a wide range of unrelated actors whose primary interests do not include the Middle East. Support from active elements in the articulate public, even those with only a peripheral interest in the issue, adds some increment of numerical and organizational weight to the group's arguments. Throughout the 1966-1974 period, pro-Israel groups were able to get leading members of the Black community, scholars, entertainers, Protestant theologians, and Catholic priests to take strong stands in favor of a pro-Israel American policy. Interest groups work hard to enlist the support of as many different segments of American society as possible in their attempts to build the appearance of a national consensus for their policy preferences, and they employ a number of tactics in order to achieve their objectives. In every phase of these endeavors pro-Israel groups have far outdistanced their pro-Arab competitors.

The most direct approach is for group leaders to lobby the leaders of other groups for endorsements of a particular policy stand. In such cases, leaders may rely on personal friendships and political log-rolling as well as the merits of their case to win outside support. A second approach is to focus propaganda efforts at large but discernible groups within society in the hope of building a broader base of mass support. During the 1966-1974 period, pro-Israel groups developed a number of programs designed to give the Israeli position on major issues to specific elements in the domestic environment. Beginning in 1969, the Presidents Conference assumed formal control of these programs, established a $25,000 per year activities budget, and hired a full-time professional coordinator to service specialized committees undertaking pro-Israel political efforts in the following sectors:

(1) campus,
(2) mass media,
(3) church bodies,
(4) the Black community, and
(5) the labor movement [Conference of Presidents, 1970: 10].

Yet another way that foreign policy groups attempt to build and maintain support from their environment is to monitor the policy stands adopted by other groups, and then publicly reinforce statements of support and refute statements of opposition. The Interreligious Affairs Department of the American Jewish Committee and the Anti-Defamation League of B'nai B'rith, for example, make periodic analyses of the public support that Israel receives from various segments of the population on both general and specific issues (see Banki, 1968; American Jewish Committee, 1971; Anti-Defamation League, 1969, 1973a, 1973b, 1974, 1975). The purpose of such activities is to keep other groups in the environment "honest;" to let them know that pro-Israel groups are sensitive to the policy stands they take on Middle East issues.

Anticipated negative reactions from the Jewish community have been a major reason why corporate actors have not taken a more active public role in the policy-making process (Quandt, 1972: 529-530). Corporate fears of an outcry from pro-Israel supporters have proved well-founded on those infrequent occasions when they have addressed the Arab-Israeli problem in the public arena. For example, a 1968 article on the conflict in the Standard Oil of New Jersey (now Exxon) publication *The Lamp* was seen by pro-Israel groups as pro-Arab and resulted in the loss of more than 200 Jewish credit card customers, and a threat of a boycott of Jersey Standard products (Quandt, 1972: 529-530). Similarly, when it became known that David Rockefeller, Chairman of the Board of the Chase Manhattan Bank, carried a message from the Egyptian government to President Nixon in December 1969, it was roundly criticized as a corporate attempt to manipulate American foreign policy. As a result, most American business leaders have assiduously avoided taking public stands on Middle East issues. A classic example of corporate shyness occurred during the 1970 hearings of the House Subcommittee on the Near East (U.S. Congress, 1970), when Charles Bonin, president of Chemical Construction Corporation (CHEMICO) and the president of the American-Arab Association for Commerce and Industry, repeatedly refused to commit himself on political issues despite prodding from subcommittee chairman L. H. Fountain (D–N.C.) and Representative John Monagan (D–Conn.):

> Mr. Fountain: Do you have any comment on the way in which the Palestinian Arabs might be brought into this picture and dealt with or consulted? How can they be brought into this overall, total effort for peace in the Middle East?
>
> Mr. Bonin: I do not believe I have any opinion or any suggestions along that line.
>
> Mr. Monagan: Mr. Bonin, you are confining yourself, in your testimony, as I take it, to the commercial and business aspects of American activity in the Arab world; is that right?
>
> Mr. Bonin: Yes.
>
> Mr. Monagan: You have not advocated removing our support.
>
> Mr. Bonin: I have not advocated removing it, increasing it, or in any way. I have not discussed support of Israel.
>
> Mr. Monagan: Are you or your conferees saying let Israel go?
>
> Mr. Bonin: Let me make clear that our association jealously guards the position that we take that we are not involved in the politics of the area. Occasionally, we have speakers who drift off into that area, and we attempt to get them back on to the business of what we call ourselves, the American Arab Association for Commerce and Industry, in which we attempt to promote the business interests of the U.S. private enterprise in the Arab world.
>
> Mr. Fountain: ... Are you saying that in the business world you are not attempting to pass judgment upon political decisions or policy decisions which our Government and other governments ought to make but that, whatever decision is made, you just want to be sure they take into account the problems and facts which you relate to us?
>
> Mr. Bonin: Yes, that is a good summary of the position we are taking.

Regardless of whether or not Mr. Bonin's testimony accurately reflects his own policy preferences, it does point out the timidity of corporations with substantial economic interests both in the United States and the Middle East to come out publicly in favor of specific policy proposals. The only corporations that see themselves as immune to domestic sanctions and therefore have not felt restrained by the implicit threat of pro-Israel retaliation for pro-Arab policy statements, are those few and relatively small American oil companies which extract, refine, and sell Arab oil abroad, and which have practically no marketing operations in the United States.

There has grown up over the years the mistaken notion that many American corporations operating in the Middle East are an integral part of the pro-Arab movement in the United States, and that some kind of pro-Arab corporate "condominium" is constantly working to bring about a pro-Arab American foreign policy in the area. However, the relationships among American corporations and pro-Arab groups are much more complex than that. The primary goal of corporations, as organizations, is to create a political and economic environment in the Middle East that will allow them to maximize profits. As such, the political interests or corporate actors are generally much narrower than those of the pro-Arab groups. Until the June War, the operations of American businesses and American foreign policy were generally viewed by American corporations and host country government officials alike as two distinct spheres of activity, and corporations had little need to engage in foreign policy activities either abroad or at home. After the June War, and even more so after the October War, some Arab governments began to tie the continued profitability, and in some cases even the existence, of American firms in the area to American governmental policy towards the conflict. As a result from 1967 on, corporate groups periodically have seen a need to remind policy-makers that deviation from an "even-handed" policy could seriously jeopardize American business operations in the Middle East.

To the extent that the economic interests of corporations have become intertwined with the political objectives of Arab governments and pro-Arab groups, there has been some potential for political cooperation. More important, there are a number of corporate executives who are ardently pro-Arab, and who, as *individuals,* could serve as links between American business and the pro-Arab movement. However, they have generally avoided assuming this role because of their differences with the most visible leaders of the pro-Arab movement, the Arab-Americans. Despite their sympathies, many pro-Arab businessmen during the 1966-1974 period refused to identify formally with any group, while others joined with leaders of American refugee aid organizations, clergymen, former government officials, university staff, and other professional types to form groups such as the Americans for Middle East Understanding who argued for an "even-handed" American policy. The result was that there developed two separate and equally weak organizational strands within the pro-Arab movement in the United States. The ties that existed between the leaders of these more "respectable" groups and corporations created both advantages and disadvantages for the pro-Arab movement as a whole. For while they tended to broaden the political base of one wing of the pro-Arab movement, they simultaneously tended to widen the divisions between the American-born and foreign-born leaders, thereby perpetuating organizational fragmentation within the movement. As a result, pro-Arab groups were unable to attain the internal cohesion and domestic support necessary to compete effectively with the pro-Israel movement.

Summary

In this section we have investigated a number of propositions derived from a general conceptual framework constructed to help us better understand the roles nongovernmental actors play in the foreign policy process and in the broader political environment that surrounds it. We have found that interest groups displayed wide variations in their influence-seeking activities. We were able to explain the behavioral variations for pro-Israel and pro-Arab groups partially in terms of differences in organizational capabilities and differences in the political support each was able to generate from other actors in the domestic political system. The pro-Israel movement's relatively more active, direct, and advocative approach to policy-making was largely a function of its numerical size, its organizational strength, and its ability to elicit widespread support for its policy positions from important segments of the articulate public. On the other hand, the pro-Arab movement's relatively less active, more indirect, and often antagonistic behavior on foreign policy issues can be attributed in part to its small size, its lack of coordination, and its isolation in a hostile or at best apathetic political environment.

Despite the importance of behavioral and strategic variables in explaining interest group impact, we have found that they are incapable by themselves of explaining the role of nongovernmental actors in the policy-making process. Because interest groups must rely on governmental actors to see their policy preferences incorporated into decisions, the receptivity and efficacy of the governmental targets selected by an interest group emerge as the most important variables determining a group's ability to affect policy. While low levels of activity, an indirect political strategy, and a generally reactive political effort are not likely to lead to a direct impact on policy, it is not always the case that an active, direct, and formulative approach will pay off in policy influence either. Rather, an aggressive political effort is a necessary but not sufficient condition for policy impact.

Dominance of policy debates in the public arena will not yield an interest group influence over foreign policy outputs if the "gate-keepers"—the policy-makers—refuse to accept the group's actions as legitimate inputs to the process, or if the group is precluded from playing a meaningful role because it is not aware that a policy-making process has even been initiated. While it is likely that pro-Israel groups played a major role in American arms sales decisions, it is equally likely that this slippage between activity and impact characterized the attempts of pro-Israel group to affect American peace-making policy. The key difference between the two issues was the strength of the pro-Israel movement's congressional allies on arms sales decisions, and their weakness relative to generally unsupportive executive actors in the formulation of American peace initiatives.

CONCLUSIONS

One of the fascinating aspects of the political process is how inputs from a wide variety of sources are blended together and then transformed into policy outputs. In this study, we have attempted to outline some of the factors that help determine the ability of interest groups to affect governmental foreign policy. We have argued that because interest groups are provided no formal role in the foreign policy process, their impact must, at minimum, be mediated by governmental actors who are willing and able to translate their preferences into governmental policy. Thus, the effects of nongovernmental inputs are likely to be less discernible and more indirect than the policy imprints of government decision-makers. Throughout the conceptual framework and the empirical analysis, we have grappled with the problem of how to dissect the impact of interest groups from the individual and combined effects of all the factors that enter into the making of foreign policy. We probably will never be able to tap all the indirect and secondary effects of nongovernmental actors on foreign policy. However, to the degree that interest groups perform the important function of generating and channeling public opinion from diverse domestic sources on foreign policy issues, and to the degree that decision-makers give the American people any say in the conduct of American foreign affairs, interest groups are likely to be guaranteed a role as catalytic agents if not primary actors in the democratic foreign policy process.

I am inclined to believe that the sustained interest of large and easily mobilized segments of the articulate public does make a difference in the way policy-makers attempt to solve foreign policy problems. To the extent that policy-makers, particularly those in the executive branch, are aware that their actions are likely to elicit some kind of reaction from interest groups, and to the degree that decision-makers anticipate public reactions and attempt to defuse criticism or elicit positive responses by selecting certain policy alternatives, interest groups are exerting an impact on policy. Admittedly, the impact of interest groups on policy outputs is very often impossible to measure. However, its incalculability makes it no less important in the study of foreign policy-making, for to focus solely on the direct effects of governmental actors is to ignore the fascinating complexity of the political process. And by overlooking the interaction effects that result from the intermingling of nongovernmental inputs during the process, we are likely to draw simplistic and erroneous conclusions that actually hinder the prospects for developing a general explanatory model of the foreign polity process.

While there are still major conceptual and empirical problems associated with understanding the role of nongovernmental actors in the policy-making

process, there is only one way that these problems will ever be resolved. More research on nongovernmental actors needs to be done, not only on their role as domestic actors in the foreign policy process, but also on their other roles as transnational linkages and as actors in policy-making processes on domestic issues. We need to examine their behavior in terms of more issues, across a broader time period, and in different countries if we are ever to be able to generalize about the role they play in the policy-making process. We must refine our conceptual frameworks and transform our propositions into testable hypotheses that can be confirmed or dismissed on the basis of empirical investigation using more systematic data. We must, in short, develop a conceptual and methodological sophistication that we presently do not possess, while keeping constant our primary commitment—not to the study of theory or methodology per se—but to the study of politics and the ways political processes affect us as human beings.

NOTES

1. Cohen (1957: 62) has described the "articulate public" in the following terms:

There is no existing terminology that satisfactorily describes this group [of politically articulate people]. The whole is obviously larger than mere "interest groups," as that term is generally employed, and yet is something less than an "opinion elite." In the absence of a suitable label we shall for convenience refer to this disparate body of organized groups and private citizens who speak out on any given issue of public policy as the "articulate public."

2. The term "linkage" is one of the most abused in the current jargon of international politics. The concept as used in this study differs considerably from that presented by Rosenau in his *Linkage Politics* (1969). Rosenau conceives of a linkage as any recurrent sequence of behavior that originates in one system and is reacted to in another. He develops a set of nine basic types of linkages, the most common of which he contends is the "fused" linkage wherein the outputs and inputs of the political systems under consideration continuously reinforce each other and are best characterized as a reciprocal relationship. There are two basic problems with Rosenau's approach to the study of linkages. First, the only characteristic used to distinguish linkage politics from other types of international political interaction is whether or not the sequences of behavior are recurrent. Almost all stable patterns of behavior between states may thus be viewed as linkages. Rosenau presents us with a matrix that displays no less than 432 areas in which national-international linkages can occur. This approach may serve to point up the fact that social scientists have for too long ignored the relationships among elements in the internal and external environments of states. However, its unnecessary complexity and the all subsuming character of its definition limit its utility as an analytical concept. Second, Rosenau's definition of the most common and important linkage, the fused linkage, is fundamentally nonoperational. As he describes it, a fused linkage is "a sequence in which an output fosters an input that in turn fosters an output in such a way that they cannot meaningfully be analyzed separately." The result is that while we may be able to assert with confidence that the interaction pattern between two polities can be characterized as a fused linkage, without the ability to separate input from output and cause from effect we have no way of explaining why or how this fused relationship has any impact on the actors' behavior. The alternative concept of linkage presented in this study hopefully will improve our capacity to understand an important yet elusive set of factors which affect the behavior and influence of nongovernmental actors.

3. Burgess and Lawton (1972: 6) describe the meaning of "events data" as follows:

> Events data is the term that has been coined to refer to words and deeds—i.e., verbal and physical actions and reactions—that international actors such as statesmen, national elites, intergovernmental organizations (IGOs), and nongovernmental international organizations (NGOs) direct toward their domestic or external environments. An event . . . is an observation of a communication process that records who says what to whom.

While the latter part of this definition fits comfortably with the types of data coded in the PANGA system, the primary focus of this study is on subnational interest groups and not on international actors.

4. There are obvious methodological problems associated with using a single data source as the basis of any behavioral analysis. In particular, we must recognize that the *New York Times* is a domestic organization whose own orientation to the Arab-Israeli situation may not always be devoid of conscious or unconscious bias. As a result, the *Times* may be "screening" some real world events that take place even in the New York area, in addition to the fact that many relevant domestic events in other parts of the United States are very likely to go unreported in the *Times*. These problems make it necessary to emphasize once again that the data used in this analysis are but a sample of all relevant events. For discussions of the strengths and weaknesses of the *New York Times Index* as an events data source see Brewer (1975); and Azar, Cohen, Jukam, and McCormick (1972).

5. Most existing international events coding systems use some variant of either the World Event/Interaction Survey (WEIS) or Corson's modified WEIS action typologies to characterize the nature of a given event. Each action is coded according to whether it reflects negative (conflictual) or positive (cooperative) affect on the part of the actor toward the target. These conflictual and cooperative acts can be verbal (accuse, approve) or non-verbal (demonstrate, consult) and they can be coded according to time (past, current, future). The problem with applying such action typologies to the domestic arena is that often the referent or subject of a given action is not the direct target of the action, in which case it becomes well nigh impossible with existing schemes to answer the question: conflictual or cooperative with regard *to what or toward whom?* See McClelland and Young (1969); and Corson (1970).

6. In terms of policy stance, a majority of the remaining 30 percent of the total events reflects the incessant squabbling that characterizes relations among pro-Israel, pro-Arab, and other groups in the United States. Thus, 9.1 percent (N=112) of the total number of events involved criticism of pro-Arab groups, 6.8 percent (N=84) centered on criticisms of pro-Israel groups, and 2.2 percent (N=27) were attacks on the policy positions of church and neutralist groups.

7. In 1972, however, a number of pro-Arab groups formed a Washington-based umbrella organization called the National Association of Arab Americans (NAAA) in an attempt to provide some coordination for pro-Arab activities in the United States. The NAAA has become increasingly active in recent years, focusing most of its attention on relevant legislation in Congress.

8. Holtzman goes on to portray the Jewish community as an illustration of his point. Needless to say, while I agree with his conceptual argument, I disagree with his supporting example.

9. Deriving a defensible measure of "influence" or "impact" remains one of the most challenging tasks facing social scientists. Most analysts still base their assessments of the extent of influence of a given actor on the perceptions of participants in the policy-making process. Despite the largely intuitive process of assigning relative strengths to domestic interest groups, there is widespread consensus that pro-Israel groups are relatively more powerful than pro-Arab groups on all issues, and that pro-Israel groups

have been relatively more influential on arms sales issues than on peace-making issues. For analyses of the impact of domestic groups on Middle East issues see Quandt (1972, 1974); Trice (1974, 1976a); Glass (1972); Rudeneh (1972); Mosher (1970); Peters (1976); and Barberis (1976).

10. It is, of course, important for us to find out why Congress is so supportive of Israel. As yet, no empirical work has been done on the sources of congressional support. As a result, we presently have a number of plausible—but untested—theories concerning why such an overwhelming percentage of lawmakers favor Israel in the conflict. For example, see Barberis (1976); Ibrahim (1974); and the American Palestine Committee (1975).

11. This finding, based on interviews with middle-ranking State Department officials in 1972-1973, supports Cohen's (1973) conclusions, which are based on interviews with State Department officials conducted in 1965-1966. In addition, interviews for this study were conducted with some 30 leaders of pro-Israel and pro-Arab groups. For a discussion of the interview techniques employed, see Trice (1974).

12. In all of the surveys questions were addressed only to informed respondents. Except for the April 1975 survey, percentages reported in the *Index* were calculated on the basis of the informed public. In the May 1975 *Index*, however, the percentages for various respondents were calculated on the basis of the total of both informed and uninformed respondents. For purposes of comparability, April 1975 responses have been recalculated as a percentage of the informed public (70 percent of all respondents) only. See *Gallup Opinion Index* (1967, 1968, 1969, 1970, 1975).

13. Particularly the American Israel Public Affairs Committee (AIPAC), the organization primarily responsible for communicating the policy preferences of organized American Jewry to members of Congress, and the Conference of Presidents of Major American Jewish Organization, which serves as the major link between organized Jewry and the executive branch.

14. Journalistic analyses of the domestic political environment on Middle East issues tend to emphasize single cause explanations for the support (or lack of it) shown for given parties to the conflict, and to advance conclusions in terms of sweeping generalizations that deemphasize the diversity of domestic opinion. For example, see *Time* (June 15, 1967; March 16, 1970; December 17, 1973); and *Congressional Quarterly* (1974). For more sophisticated analyses see Raab (1974); and Harris (1975).

REFERENCES

ALLISON, G. T. (1971) Essence of Decision: Explaining the Cuban Missile Crisis. Boston: Little, Brown.

——— and M. H. HALPERIN (1972) "Bureaucratic politics: a paradigm and some policy implications," pp. 40-79 in R. Tanter and R. H. Ullman (eds.) Theory and Policy in International Relations. Princeton: Princeton Univ. Press.

ALMOND, G. A. (1958) "Research note: a comparative study of interest groups and the political process." Amer. Pol. Sci. Rev., LII, 1 (March): 270-282.

ALTER, R. (1970) "Zionism for the 70's." Commentary (February): 47-57.

——— (1968) "Rhetoric and the Arab mind." Commentary (October): 61.

American Histadrut Cultural Exchange Institute (1969) The Impact of Israel on American Jewry: A Symposium. New York.

American Institute for Political Communication (1967) Domestic Communications Aspects of the Middle East Crisis. Washington, D.C. (July).

American Jewish Committee (1971) Christians Support Unified Jerusalem. New York.

——— (1969) Arab Appeals to American Public Opinion Today. New York.

American Palestine Committee (1975) "The payoff." Southbury, Conn.

Anti-Defamation League of B'nai B'rith (1975) "Big 50 press survey: the suspension of Middle East negotiations" (April).

--- (1974) "U.S. press reaction to Arafat's U.N. speech" (December).
---(1973a) "American press reaction to the Mideast conflict" (November).
--- (1973b) "Negative reactions to Israel's plight" (November).
--- (1973c) "The response of American institutional life to the Middle East crisis" (November).
Arab Information Center (1972) Who Says What to Whom. New York.
ART, R. J. (1973) "Bureaucratic politics and American foreign policy: a critique." Policy Sciences, IV: 467-490.
AVINERI, S. (1971) "The New Left and Israel," pp. 293-302 in M. Curtis (ed.) People and politics in the Middle East. New Brunswick, N.J.: Transaction.
AZAR, E. (1975) "Ten issues in events research," pp. 1-23, in E. Azar and J. Ben-Dak (eds.) Theory and Practice of Events Research. New York: Gordon & Breach.
--- and J. BEN-DAK (1975) Theory and Practice of Events Research. New York: Gordon & Breach.
AZAR, E., R. BRODY and C. McCLELLAND (1972) International Events Interaction Analysis. Sage Professional Papers in International Studies, 1, 02-001. Beverly Hills and London: Sage Pub.
AZAR, E., S. COHEN, T. JUKAM and J. McCORMICK (1972) "The problem of source coverage in the use of international events data," International Studies Q., 16 (September): 373-388.
BANKI, J. H. (1968) Christian Reactions to the Middle East Crisis. New York: American Jewish Committee.
BARBERIS, M. (1976) "The Arab-Israeli battle on Capitol Hill," Virginia Q. Rev., 52 (Spring): 202-223.
BAUER, R. A., I. POOL, and L. A. DEXTER (1963) American Business and Public Policy: The Politics of Foreign Trade. New York: Atherton.
BLAISDELL, D. C. [ed.] (1958) Unofficial Government: Pressure Groups and Lobbies. Annals of the Amer. Academy of Pol. and Soc. Science (September).
BONILLA, F. (1956) "When is petition 'pressure'?" Public Opinion Q. XX, 1 (Spring): 39-47.
BRECHER, M. (1971) The Foreign Policy System of Israel. New Haven: Yale Univ. Press.
--- B. STEINBERG, and J. STEIN (1969) "A framework for research on foreign policy behavior." J. of Conflict Resolution, XIII, 1 (March): 75-101.
BREWER, T. (1975) "Foreign policy process events," pp. 197-215 in E. Azar and J. Ben-Dak (eds.) Theory and Practice of Events Research. New York: Gordon & Breach.
BURDETTE, F. (1958) "Influence of non-congressional pressures on foreign policy." Annals of the Amer. Academy of Pol. and Soc. Science (September): 92-99.
BURGESS, P. and R. LAWTON (1972) Indicators of International Behavior. Sage Professional Papers International Studies, 1, 02-010. Beverly Hills and London: Sage Pub.
CAMPBELL, J. D. (1970) "The Arab-Israeli conflict: an American Policy." Foreign Affairs (October): 51-69.
CELLER, E. (1958) "Pressure groups in Congess." Annals of the Amer. Academy of Pol. and Soc. Science (September): 1-9.
CHITTICK, W. O. (1970) State Department, Press, and Pressure Groups: A Role Analysis. New York: Wiley.
COHEN, B. C. (1973) The Public's Impact on Foreign Policy. Boston: Little, Brown.
--- (1959) The Influence of Non-governmental Groups on Foreign Policy-making. Boston: World Peace Foundation.
--- (1957) The Political Process and Foreign Policy: The Making of the Japanese Peace Settlement. Princeton: Princeton Univ. Press.
Conference of Presidents of Major American Jewish Organizations (1966-1975) Report for the Year. New York.

—— (1967) Days of Crisis: April 1 to September 30, 1967; A President's Conference Interim Report. New York.
Congressional Quarterly (1974) The Middle East: U.S. Policy, Israel, Oil and the Arabs. Washington, D.C.
CORSON, W. (1970) "Conflict and cooperation in East-West relations: measurement and explanation." Paper presented at annual meeting of Amer. Pol. Sci. Assn.
DEAN, J. P., and W. F. WHYTE (1970) "How do you know if the informant is telling the truth?" in L. A. Dexter (ed.) Elite and Specialized Interviewing. Evanston, Ill.: Northwestern Univ. Press.
DEXTER, L. A. (1969) How Organizations are Represented in Washington. Indianapolis: Bobbs-Merrill.
EHRMANN, H. W. [ed.] (1958) Interest Groups on Four Continents. Pittsburgh: Univ. of Pittsburgh Press.
ELDERSVELD, S. J. (1958) "American interest groups: a survey of research and some implications for theory and method," pp. 173-196 in H. W. Ehrmann (ed.) Interest Groups on Four Continents. Pittsburgh: Univ. of Pittsburgh Press.
ELLIS, H. B. (1964) "The Arab-Israeli conflict today," pp. 113-147 in G. Stevens (ed.) The United States and the Middle East. Englewood Cliffs, N.J.: Prentice-Hall.
ENGLER, R. (1961) The Politics of Oil: Private Power and Democratic Directions. Chicago: Univ. of Chicago Press.
ERSKINE, H. (1969-1970) "The polls: western partisanship in the Middle East." Public Opinion Q. XXXIII, 4 (Winter): 627-640.
ETZIONI, A. (1966) Studies in Social Change. New York: Holt, Rinehart & Winston.
FELD, W. (1972) Non-governmental Forces and World Politics: A Study of Business, Labor, and Political Groups. New York: Praeger.
FINE, M., and M. HIMMELFARB [eds.] (1966-1964) The American Jewish Yearbook. New York: American Jewish Committee and American Jewish Pub. Soc. of America.
FRIEDMAN, N. L. (1969) "Problem of the runaway Jewish intellectuals: social definition and sociological perspective." Jewish Social Studies (January): 3-19.
Friends Peace and International Relations Committee and Friends Service Council (1970) Search for Peace in the Middle East: A Quaker Study. London.
GABLE, R. W. (1958) "Interest groups as policy shapers." Annals of the Amer. Academy of Pol. and Soc. Science (September): 84-93.
GALLUP, G. and J. DAVIES (1971) "Religion in America." Gallup Opinion Ineex, Report 70 (April).
Gallup Opinion Index (1967-1975) Princeton (Report 25, July 1967; Report 38, August 1968; Report 44, February 1969; Report 58, April 1970; Report 119, May 1975).
GERSHMAN, C. (1975) The Foreign Policy of American Labor. The Washington Papers, III, 29. Beverly Hills and London: Sage Pub.
GLASS, A. J. (1972) "Nixon gives Israel massive aid but reaps no Jewish political harvest." National Report, IV, 2 (January 8): 56.
GLAZER, N. (1969) "Blacks, Jews and the intellectuals." Commentary (April): 33-39.
GOLDMAN, N. (1970) "The future of Israel." Foreign Affairs, XXXVIII, 3 (April): 443-459.
GOODMAN, W. (1971) "I'd love to see the JDL fold up. But . . ." New York Times Mag. (November 21): 33.
HALPERIN, S. (1961) The Political World of American Zionism. Detroit: Wayne State Press.
HALPERIN, M. H. and A. KANTER (1973) "The bureaucratic perspective: a preliminary framework," pp. 1-42 in M. H. Halperin and A. Kanter (eds.) Readings in American Foreign Policy. Boston: Little, Brown.
HAMMOND, P. Y. and S. S. ALEXANDER [eds] (1972) Political Dynamics in the Middle East. New York: American Elsevier Pub.
HARRIS, L. (1975) "Oil or Israel?" New York Times Mag. (April 6): 22.

HERMANN, C. F. (1971) "What is a foreign policy event?" pp. 295-321 in W. Hanreider (ed.) Comparative Foreign Policy. New York: McKay.

HERSHBERG, M. A. (1973) "Ethnic interest groups and foreign policy: a case study of the activities of the organized Jewish community in regard to the 1968 decision to sell Phantom jets to Israel." Univ. of Pettsburgh: Unpub. dis.

HIMMELFARB, M. (1969) "Is American Jewry in crisis?" Commentary (March): 33-42.

HOLTZMAN, A. (1966) Interest Groups and Lobbying. New York: Macmillan.

HUFF, E. (1972) "A study of a successful interest group: the American Zionist movement." Western Pol. Q., XXV, 1 (March): 109-124.

HUREWITZ, J. C. [ed.] (1976) Oil, the Arab-Israel Dispute, and the Industrial World: Horizons of Crisis. Boulder, Col.: Westview.

IBRAHIM, S. (1974) "American domestic forces and the October War." J. of Palestine Studies, IV (Autumn): 55-81.

Israel Ministry for Foreign Affairs (1972) Accessories to Terror: The Responsibility of Arab Governments for the Organization of Terrorist Activities. Jerusalem.

JABARA, A. (1970) "The legalities of a tax-exempt and tax-deductible status for Zionist-Israeli colonization of Palestine," pp. 126-152 in Naseer Aruri (ed.) The Palestinian Resistance to Israeli Occupation. Wilmette, Ill.: Medina Univ. Press Internatl.

KAHANE, M. (1971) Never Again: A Program for Survival. Los Angeles: Nash.

KASHEF, A. R. (1970) "United States assistance to Israel: the military dimension" in The United States, Israel and the Arab States. Information Paper 3. Chicago: Assn. of Arab-American University Graduates.

KEY, V. O. (1942) Politics, Parties and Pressure Groups. New York: Crowell.

KEY, V. O., Jr. (1961) Public Opinion and American Democracy. New York: Knopf.

KIMCHE, D. and D. BAWLEY (1968) The Sandstorm: The Arab Israeli War of June 1967: Prelude and Aftermath. London: Secker & Warburg.

KOEHANE, R. O., and J. S. NYE, Jr. [eds.] (1972) Transnational Relations and World Politics. Cambridge: Harvard Univ. Press.

KRAFT, J. (1971) "Those Arabists in the State Department." New York Times Mag. (November 7): 38.

LaPALOMBARA, J. (1964) Interest Groups in Italian Politics. Princeton: Princeton Univ. Press.

LAQUEUR, W. (1972) A History of Zionism. New York: Holt, Rinehart & Winston.

--- R. ALTER, and N. GLAZER (1971) "Revolutionism and the Jews." Commentary (February): 38-61.

LEVY, M. R. and M. S. KRAMER (1975) "The ethnic vote," pp. 111-140 in R. Reilly and M. Sigall (eds.) New Patterns in American Politics. New York: Praeger.

LIPSET, S. M. (1971) "Socialism of fools: the New Left calls it anti-Zionism." New York Times Mag. (January 31): 39; (March 14): 16.

--- (1969) "Left, the Jews and Israel." Encounter (December): 24-25.

MALLISON, W. T., Jr. (1968) "The legal problems concerning the juridical status and political activities of the Zionist organization/Jewish agency: a study in international and United States law." William and Mary Law Rev. 9, 556. Williamsburg, Va.: 554-629.

--- (1964) "The Zionist-Israel juridical claims to constitute 'The Jewish People' nationality entity and to confer membership in it: appraisal in public international law." George Washington Law Rev., XXXII, 5. Washington, D.C. (June): 983-1075.

MANSBACH, R. and D. LAMPERT (1975) "The nonstate actor project." International Studies Notes, 2 (Fall): 1-13.

MASLOW, W. (1961) "The legal defense of religious liberty—the strategy and tactics of the American Jewish Congress." Paper presented to Amer. Pol. Sci. Assn. meeting.

McCLELLAND, C. A. and R. A. YOUNG (1970) "The flow of international events, July-December 1969." World Event/Interaction Survey Interim Report. Univ. of Southern California (January).

McGOWAN, P. J. (1970) "The unit-of-analysis problem in the comparative study of foreign policy." Paper prepared for Events Data Measurement Conference, Michigan State Univ., East Lansing, Mich. (April).
MILBRATH, L. (1967) "Interest groups and foreign policy," pp. 231-252 in J. Rosenau (ed.) Domestic Sources of Foreign Policy. New York: Free Press.
MOSHER, L. (1970) "Zionist role in U.S. raises new concern." National Observer (May 18).
NES, D. (1972) "Israel and the American election." Middle East International (October): 10.
PERLMUTTER, A. (1971) "The fiasco of Anglo-American Middle East policy," pp. 220-249 in M. Curtis (ed.) People and Politics in the Middle East. New Brunswick, N.J.: Transaction.
PETERS, C. (1976) "Lobbies and their influence on government," pp. 137-179 in C. Peters and J. Fallows (eds.) The System: The Five Branches of American Government. New York: Praeger.
PHILLIPS, W. R. (1974) "Theoretical underpinnings of the event data movement." Paper presented at Annual Meeting of the Internatl. Studies Assn., New York.
PORTER, K. H., and D. B. JOHNSON [eds.] (1970) National Party Platforms, 1840-1968. Urbana, Ill.: Univ. of Illinois Press.
QUANDT, W. (1974) "The Arab-Israeli conflict in American foreign policy." Paper presented to North American Study Group on the Middle East, New York (December).
--- (1973) "Domestic influences on United States foreign policy in the Middle East: the view from Washington," pp. 264-285 in W. Beling (ed.) The Middle East: Quest for an American Policy. Albany, N.Y.: State Univ. of New York Press.
--- (1972) "United States policy in the Middle East," pp. 489-532 in P. Hammond and S. Alexander (eds.) Political Dynamics in the Middle East. New York: Elsevier.
RAAB, E. (1974) "Is Israel losing popular support?" Commentary (January): 26-29.
--- (1970) "Deadly innocence of American Jews." Commentary (December): 31-29.
ROSENAU, J. N. (1973a) "Mobilizing the attentive citizen: a model and some data on a neglected dimension of political participation." Paper presented at 1973 annual meeting of the Ameri. Pol. Sci. Assn., New Orleans (September).
--- (1973b) "Theorizing across systems: linkage politics revisited," pp. 25-58 in J. Wilkenfeld (ed.) Conflict Behavior and Linkage Politics. New York: David McKay.
--- (1969) Linkage Politics: Essays on the Convergence of National and International Systems. New York: Free Press.
--- (1968) "Moral fervor, systematic analysis, and scientific consciousness in foreign policy research," pp. 197-225 in A. Ranney (ed.) Political Science and Public Policy. Chicago: Markham.
--- (1963) National Leadership and Foreign Policy: A Case Study in the Mobilization of Public Support. Princeton, N.J.: Princeton Univ. Press.
RUBIN, J. A. (1969) Partners in State-Building: American Jewry and Israel. New York: Diplomatic Press.
RUDENEH, O. (1972) "The Jewish factor in U.S. politics." J. of Palestine Studies, 1 (Summer): 92-107.
SAFRAN, N. (1974) "Engagement in the Middle East." Foreign Affairs, 53 (October): 45-63.
--- (1969) From War to War: The Arab-Israel Confrontation, 1948-1967. New York: Pegasus.
SALISBURY, R. (1975) "Interest groups," pp. 171-228 in F. Greenstein and N. Polsby (eds.) Handbook of Political Science, Vol. 4. Boston: Addison-Wesley.
SAYRE, W. S. and H. KAUFMAN (1960, 1965) Governing New York City: Politics in the Metropolis. New York: Norton.
SCHECHTMAN, J. B. (1966) The United States and the Jewish State Movement, the Crucial Decade: 1939-1949. New York: Thomas Yoseloff.

SILVERBERG, R. (1970) If I Forget Thee O Jerusalem: American Jews and the State of Israel. New York: Morrow.
SINGER, I. B. (1967) "Extreme Jews." Harpers (April): 55-62.
SNYDER, R. C., H. W. BRUCK, and B. SAPIN (1962) "Decision-making as an approach to the study of international politics" in R. C. Snyder, H. W. Bruck, and B. Sapin (eds.) Foreign Policy Decision-making. Glencoe, Ill.: Free Press.
SOLOWAY, A. M., E. WEISS, and G. COPLAN (1971) Truth and Peace in the Middle East: A Critical Analysis of the Quaker Report. New York: Friendly House.
SPIEGEL, S. L. (1973) "The fate of the patron: American trials in the Arab-Israeli dispute." Public Policy, XXI (Spring): 173-201.
——— (1972) "The dominant and the subordinate system: the patrons versus the pygmies in the Middle East." Paper presented at 1972 annual meeting of the Amer. Pol. Sci. Assn., Washington, D.C. (September).
STEVENS, G. G. [ed.] (1964) The United States and the Middle East. Englewood Cliffs, N.J.: Prentice-Hall.
TANZER, M. (1969) The Political Economy of International Oil and the Underdeveloped Countries. Boston: Beacon.
TRICE, R. H. (1976a) "American interest groups after October 1973," pp. 79-95 in J. C. Hurewitz (ed.) Oil, the Arab-Israel Dispute, and the Industrial World. Boulder, Col.: Westview.
——— (1976b) "The political activities of non-governmental actors (PANGA) project: codebook and manual." (mimeo). Columbus, Ohio.
——— (1974) Domestic Political Interests and American Policy in the Middle East. Univ. of Wisconsin-Madison: Unpub. dis.
TRUMAN, D. B. (1951, 1971) The Governmental Process: Political Interests and Public Opinion. New York: Knopf.
TURNER, H. A. (1958) "How pressure groups operate." Annals of the Amer. Academy of Pol. and Soc. Science (September): 63-72.
ULLMAN, R. (1975) "After Rabat: Middle East risks and American roles." Foreign Affairs, 53 (January): 284-296.
U.S. Congress (1971) The Middle East, 1971: The Need to Strengthen the Peace. Hearings, Subcommittee on the Near East of the Com. on Foreign Affairs, House of Rep., 92nd Congress, 1st Sess.
——— (1970) The Near East Conflict. Hearings, Subcommittee of the Near East of the Com. on Foreign Affairs, House of Rep., 91st Congress, 2nd Sess.
——— (1963) Activities of Nondiplomatic Representatives of Foreign Principals in the United States. Hearings, Senate Com. on Foreign Relations, 88th Congress, 1st Sess.
WAGNER, C. H. (1973) "Elite American newspaper opinion and the Middle East: commitment versus isolation" in W. A. Beling (ed.) The Middle East: Quest for an American Policy. Albany, N.Y.: State Univ. of New York Press.
WARWICK, D. P. (1972) "Transnational participation and international peace," pp. 305-324 in R. Keohane and J. Nye (eds.) Transnational Relations and World Politics. Cambridge, Mass.: Harvard Univ. Press.
WRIGHT, C. R. and H. HYMAN (1958) "Voluntary memberships of American adults: evidence from national sample surveys." Amer. Soc. Rev., XXIII, 2 (June): 284-292.
WILKENFELD, J. [ed.] (1973) Conflict Behavior and Linkage Politics. New York: David McKay.
WYNN, M. (1973) The Event Data Approach to Political Research: A Bibliography. Arlington, Va.: C.A.C.I.
——— and M. SMITH (1973) The International and Domestic Event Coding System: INDECS. Arlington, Va.: C.A.C.I.
ZAMIL, A. A. (1973) The Effectiveness and Credibility of Arab Propganda in the United States. Univ. of Southern California: Unpub. dis.
ZEIGLER, H. (1964) Interest Groups in American Society. Englewood Cliffs, N.J.: Prentice-Hall.

ABOUT THIS SERIES

Ordering Information

As separates:

Papers may be purchased separately for $3.00 each. Orders totaling less than $10.00 must be accompanied by payment. If you wish to receive announcements about forthcoming titles in the Sage Professional Papers series, please send your name and address to: SAGE PROFESSIONAL PAPERS IN INTERNATIONAL STUDIES, Sage Publications (address below).

On subscription:

Subscriptions are available on a volume basis. A volume consists of eight separately bound papers offered at $21.00 per volume.

N.B. All prices subject to change without notice.

ORDER FROM

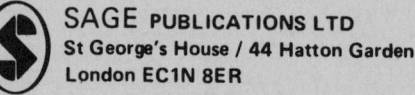

SAGE PUBLICATIONS, INC.
275 South Beverly Drive
Beverly Hills, California 90212

SAGE PUBLICATIONS LTD
St George's House / 44 Hatton Garden
London EC1N 8ER

DAVIDSON   GROUPS/FOREIGN POLICY
$3.00

SAGE PUBLICATIONS, INC.
275 South Beverly Drive
Beverly Hills, California 90212

SAGE PUBLICATIONS LTD
St George's House / 44 Hatton Garden
London EC1N 8ER